ASSARACUS

A JOURNAL OF GAY AND QUEER POETRY

26

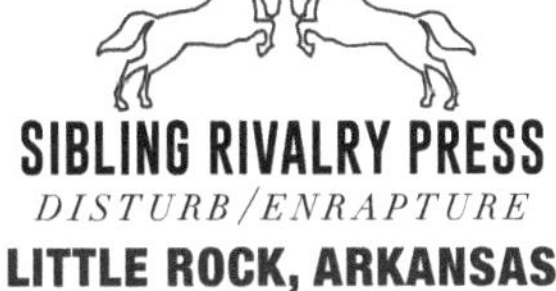

SIBLING RIVALRY PRESS

DISTURB/ENRAPTURE

LITTLE ROCK, ARKANSAS

Cover image: "Boy Area" by Cash.
Used with permission.

In the wise words of Kazim Ali, "To love one another in the world is what we are meant to do. Not war, not genocide, not dispossession and greed. There is enough for everyone. People are important, not religions or governments or gods and kings. Figs. Kisses. Books. Kindness. It's radical to love and to live so others can also live and love."

Sibling Rivalry Press
159 Sunset Drive
North Little Rock, AR 72118
info@siblingrivalrypress.com
www.siblingrivalrypress.com

Printed in the United States of America.

Founding Editor: Bryan Borland
www.bryanborland.com

ISBN: 978-1-943977-87-1
ISSN: 2159-0478

Assaracus Issue 26: A Journal of Gay and Queer Poetry
October 2025.

IF YOU ARE NOT QUEER
QUEER POETRY
IS NOT YOUR
SAFE SPACE.
YOU ARE WELCOME
BUT YOUR COMFORT
IS NOT OUR PRIORITY.

OUR JOY IS.
OUR SEX IS.
OUR ART IS.
OUR LIVES ARE.
OUR SURVIVAL IS.

COVER PHOTOGRAPH BOY AREA by CASH

CASH IS A SELF-TAUGHT PHOTOGRAPHER BASED IN SAN FRANCISCO AND RECOGNIZED FOR HIS ABILITY TO CREATE HONEST, CINEMATIC IMAGES THAT RESONATE WITH VIEWERS. ORIGINALLY FROM ARKANSAS, HE HAS BEEN SHAPED MORE BY LIFE EXPERIENCES THAN BY FORMAL EDUCATION. CASH INITIALLY FOCUSED ON ARCHITECTURAL PHOTOGRAPHY BEFORE DISCOVERING HIS TRUE PASSION FOR CAPTURING THE ESSENCE OF INDIVIDUALS. HIS WORK EMPHASIZES GENUINE MOMENTS, THE USE OF NATURAL LIGHT, AND FOSTERING THE ATMOSPHERE WHERE EACH SUBJECT FEELS COMFORTABLE AND BEAUTIFUL IN THEIR OWN SKIN. WHETHER HE IS ENGAGED IN PORTRAITURE, EDITORIAL PROJECTS, OR FINE ART, CASH APPROACHES EACH SESSION WITH EMPATHY, CURIOSITY, AND A STRAIGHTFORWARD METHODOLOGY, STRIVING TO CONVEY AUTHENTIC STORIES WITHOUT PRETENSE.
INSTAGRAM = @CASHONLYPHOTOS

FEATURING

IN MEMORY OF RUSSELL BUNGE
WHO LOVED GAY POETRY
AND WHO ALWAYS SHOWED UP

CHEN CHEN
COCK = AIR

CHEN CHEN IS THE AUTHOR OF TWO BOOKS OF POETRY, *YOUR EMERGENCY CONTACT HAS EXPERIENCED AN EMERGENCY* **(2022) AND** *WHEN I GROW UP I WANT TO BE A LIST OF FURTHER POSSIBILITIES* **(2017), BOTH PUBLISHED BY BOA EDITIONS. HIS LATEST CHAPBOOK IS** *EXPLODINGLY YOURS* **(GHOST CITY PRESS, 2023). HIS HONORS INCLUDE THE THOM GUNN AWARD, THREE PUSHCART PRIZES, THE NATIONAL BOOK AWARD LONGLIST, AND FELLOWSHIPS FROM KUNDIMAN, THE NATIONAL ENDOWMENT FOR THE ARTS, AND UNITED STATES ARTISTS. HE LIVES IN ROCHESTER, NEW YORK, AND TEACHES FOR THE MFA PROGRAM AT NEW ENGLAND COLLEGE.**

TALE OF THE HAYLOFT

"Hayloft"—what a beautiful word
I don't think I have ever used, & in all likelihood never will, as I am a city
gay & have not once lofted hay nor do I have any interest
in the practice or the concept.

Never use the word, though?
Never ever utter it?
Why not turn to the person sitting to my left at this poetry reading,
this gentleman who is, most likely, a poet, too (look
at his tote bag), & there's a not small chance he's gay, too (look
at his other tote bag) (or just the fact
that he's here) so why not
ask him, Hey,

"hayloft"—what do you think about that word?
Isn't it beautiful? Or do you find it
just okay?
Do you, oh gosh, hate it?

Actually, it would be great if you hated it, as lately I've been trying
not to hate when someone is not
exactly the gay poet I am, loving
exactly the gay words I do, as I'd love
to become more capable of letting in other people,
other realities & their motley
multitude of totes.

So, please, yes, hate "hayloft." Hate it or feel
anything about it, feel
nothing towards it with all the golden hay
in your lovely loft.
& tell me why you feel
that way, please, the whole wildly *you* story, Mister Gentleman,
I don't think the reading is starting yet,
if it ever will.

PERFECT DAY

after Perfect Days (2023)
with thanks to Michael, Sarah, Christopher, & Andy

I woke up sad. Skipped breakfast.
Thought about my sadness, the thing making me sad, my sad
room led sadly to more thinking, & then I was angry
I was still sad by lunchtime.
Still sad after months since the sad thing happened.
& it felt pointless to talk about.
I tried to remind myself:
just as your day can be ruined at any moment,
a perfect day can start at any time.
So, I went on the hike with the other writers in the early afternoon.
Sad & skeptical that the hike would lessen it.
Sad while getting mud on my shoes & mosquito bites
on my hands. Sad but enjoying the conversation about dragonflies
& the movement through the woods, careful
not to step on any dragonflies, though it made me sad
to learn that they eat butterflies.
Sad but the other writers were getting bit, too.
Except Christopher.
Lucky Christopher, though later he said he felt left out,
& that was nice.
It was very nice of Christopher
to drive us to the ice cream place, where I realized
it had been a minute since I had ice cream, maybe a year, & forever
since I had it in a cone.
We ate our ice cream on little benches while looking out
at big mountains. Maybe everyone in some way
was sad, but right now we just wanted to smile & talk about how good
our treat was.
Ice cream in cones!
& then we didn't smile or say anything at all
because it was that good.

MEREDITH JULIA STARKMAN

Is this for real?
Is that a legit charge?
Don't underestimate her.
She is the red
plume at the heart of the lava
lamp in this world
that does not coo enough,
it simply does not. See this
merengue? Its stiff peaks
capable of being super
upside down?
Yeah. That's her soul.
& she's taking it
on a brisk walk.
Where are they going?
Who are they meeting?
Dunno. But they're going
to get there. They're going
to meet them. Maybe it's
a big curvy rock
in Joshua Tree.
Maybe a pig
also in Joshua Tree.
Or, a typewriter
in the middle of a very
old-school back to school
sale at Target.
Don't be cool,
says her soul, Be
a magnet for coos
& uncouth clacking.

TALE OF THE READER & THE WATCHER

All afternoon I've been on the couch, tearing
off small, terribly
irregular pieces of an ugly postcard. They've been turning

into bookmarks for a large Selected by a poet
sort of famous & recently dead. The postcard (a gift
kind of) features a campus
to which I'd once been invited to talk. The college
isn't ugly, but the very large typeface
declaring its name over the whole thing
is. A bad face,
something I would never say about a person

except gay men I find annoying. Still,
I wouldn't be tearing up this postcard
that was collecting dust on a side table, except I'm
too lazy to retrieve my post-its from upstairs, & I
despise dogearing.
This is the creature I am. I want a long life. I want

to start a sentence with "I desire" instead of "I want."
I desire a short break from my reading
& postcard-shredding. I take it.
A vital recess. Then I pause my phone, the video
of an orgy of ten men—in order

to read ten more poems. I am challenging myself again
to maintain balance.

Of course, the video keeps playing in my head as I read.
For a while there were only
eight men. Then I got confused.
I must've skipped the part where the last two joined,
though they made little difference.
After the ten poems, the ten men look uglier,

but the sex is hotter.
Three of the poems are about a man's touch. The rest,
the moon in Greece.

(I tear off another two shards of postcard.)

Poems know: try as one might to put the moon in Greece
on postcards, one can't.
You have to go there. A poem can get close.

I have not been to Greece. I'm not sure if I desire an orgy
in actuality. The videos of them seem overly choreographed
& not choreographed enough.
Toward the end of this scene one of the men
falls off a large table.
I'm surprised the director kept this in. I worry

for the man's penis before I worry for his face.
Probably it's time for an eleventh poem.
But the truly shocking part is how his fall
isn't as comical as him

getting back up on the table. He looks
so confused; perhaps he, too, needs to recount the men.

I think the director kept this in
because it's funny & the man is
beautiful as he's looking all around the room
that must now be pungent,
trying to remember who to suck or fuck next. He looks
exceedingly beautiful, but I do not desire

to have to keep track like that.
I desire to put this moment on a postcard
to send to my best friend, though none of these men
are hairy enough for him. Maybe

I just want to watch orgies, on my computer or
in a nightclub backroom or in somebody's large enough
living room.
Maybe all of the above.
I want a long, long life, & at the end I want to say

life's too short. Not because I'm afraid to die but because
I still like living. I hope

I go out noticing something, seeing a thing for the first time,
& being surprised by it
in a good way, while my lover says,
God, I wish he weren't making that face.

COCKSONG

Cock as liberation. Cock as totality. Cockful
immersion is ultimate meditation. Cock = air. Cock =
the dizzy fun lack. Soft cock?
Such geography of sway. Hard cock? What topography of vein. Cock:
musk map to the fag stars. Cock—
the usual culprit behind the word "tumescence." Workers of the cock,
let's wank! Cockily
& ballsily. Cockslut in a LaGuardia restroom. Cocksulk
at the languid picnic. Cocksong
through the wormhole. Cock as rest. Cock
is what best rhymes with cock. Two cocks
are a chant. Three or more cocks...
a chorus, a debate, a rut ruckus, a state, a frot circus, a critique
of a dissertation on the movement to completely recockify cock.

TALE OF THE POEM & THE CHAIR

after a poem & a chair I met at Brooklyn Poets

There was a poem sitting in a broken chair.
It was written from the perspective
of the broken chair. Or it was written
by the broken chair, warning of the sorrow, the fall
that would befall any would-be sitter.

Blank back straight against the chair, the poem sat
with better posture than most people.
It was accompanied by another sheet of paper,
lying on the seat, which simply read
DO NOT SIT
in case the poem was not enough to dissuade
or a reader did not have the patience to sit with it.
Or, this was a two-part poem, wistful
then commanding.

The chair, meanwhile, was very green & looked
only a little broken, but that was enough
to be dangerous to sit in, the way
a heart only a bit broken
can be dangerous to walk around with,
so it is often recommended to sit & read something,
or just sit, that can be very good, too.

Perhaps the poem was a way for the chair to sit
in its own brokenness.

Was it dangerous for the poem to sit there?
Physically, not likely.
Spiritually, maybe.
In any case, it went on sitting, & seemed

more beautiful the more you looked at it,
not because of what it said, but because of how
it sat—lightly, gently, almost nothing,
like a sheet of air
in its broken chair.

KEVIN JOSEPH BERTOLERO

Oh, you party person. So good
at making QR codes & remembering
your umbrella, so party. You know
it's not publish or perish, it's publish
& party. How likeable. Is it possible
to be kind of too likeable, personable?
Personally, you kind of are. Even or
especially tonight, with you bringing
your heaps of homework to the pizza
party, the post-reading afterparty.
You are trying to complete
the assignment one of us at this wildest
of writing conferences gave earlier:
to make a poem using words
that use only the letters in your name.
O Kevin Joseph Bertolero.
The way you move your body
over dozens of small white rectangles,
each inscribed with a single word
in neat all-caps handwriting, no,
no one says this anymore but
it is penmanship.
You are building a poem. & we
have gathered around you with our
pepperoni & plain cheese & vegan
to watch. It's mesmerizing. This
process. Your personality. I can use
penis! you shout. Meaning the word
penis. Though you would prefer dick
or cock. You are gay. Many of us
are gay. All of us agree that
in the gay poet afterlife, you would
be the life of that afterparty,
surrounded by fellow art maniacs
& enjambment fags
because you know how to find
your people. We who can't stop
recommending the best bookstore

in Minneapolis, the best bad movie
after a breakup, the best episode
of *Buffy* featuring a conversation
between Spike & Willow. You know
everyone becomes more likeable
the more they find something
& another thing to like about
each other. A common enemy, sure,
right (Riley), but you'd rather bring us
together around a word, like pole,
like hole, like ooh, jerk, vein, stroke, bro,
kiss, knob, lover, role, slobber, toes, pine,
probe, top, lips, job, penis, eros, or
phist with a ph. Who could've known
your name contained an entire gay
lexicon? Such a hot cosmos? Imagine
being Kevin. A few of us do, are
envious. But we can't help
but put that aside. Giggly fun
is far more beautiful. Friendship
growing? Even better.

DREAM JOB

The boss said, Dream about Eternity
but who wants to do that.
I dreamt about kissing
& not for Eternity, not
even "all night"
because that would get annoying,
but for a decently long time.
Lots of gay kissing.
Then, walking around the Bund
in Shanghai again, & a few other activities.
& when I woke up, my free time
said, Nothing can make up for
what your parents did to you,
they can't make it up. But
with them, now, slowly,
you can make a sort of way.
It was a message of Love.
It was nauseating.
I couldn't wait to get back to work.

DANIEL DIAMOND
MALE RAIN

DANIEL DIAMOND WAS BORN IN MICHIGAN AND MOVED TO NEW YORK CITY IN 1972. BEFORE HIS DEATH FROM AIDS IN 1996, HE PUBLISHED AT LEAST A DOZEN POETRY CHAPBOOKS; THE POEMS PUBLISHED HERE COMPRISE THE ORIGINAL TEXT OF *MALE RAIN* **(1982). DIAMOND'S SELECTED POEMS WILL APPEAR IN LATE 2026 FROM REBEL SATORI PRESS. THIS VOLUME WILL BE EDITED BY PHILIP CLARK, WHO PREVIOUSLY CO-EDITED THE ANTHOLOGY** *PERSISTENT VOICES: POETRY BY WRITERS LOST TO AIDS* **AND COLLECTIONS OF WORK BY DONALD BRITTON AND WALTA BORAWSKI. THANKS TO JERRY ROSCO, DIAMOND'S LITERARY EXECUTOR, FOR PERMISSION TO REPRINT, AND TO IAN YOUNG FOR BIBLIOGRAPHICAL ASSISTANCE.**

'GAY' AT THIRTY

I tuned into the Dick Cavett Show. John Simon,
Cavett's guest, was lamenting the loss of the word 'gay,'
(to mean "happily excited" or "bright and lively"
or "brilliant in color") from today's English.

I looked in my dog-eared, second-hand dictionary
and found another meaning: "given to social pleasures,
licentious." Surely, this was one origin of the current
politically-charged meaning the little word 'gay' had,
a meaning I doubted it would soon lose.

Later that evening, walking down Broadway, I considered
the word 'gay' in relation to myself for the first time.
Until I saw him I'd only wanted women. Sex with them
was like dreaming in a rocking chair or diving
into a geyser just as it becomes a cool pond or hearing
a duet for cello and trumpet. From puberty, only
the yielding but resistant bodies of women excited me.

Walking along Broadway in the twilight, maybe it was
the damp tee-shirt hugging his chest, the pungence
of his sweat as he jogged past, or the memory of every
gym coach I'd looked up to, every buddy I'd played ball
or camped out with, even the fag intellectual we'd
snapped with our wet towels in the locker room, but
suddenly, I wanted to taste a man.

Now that I have, I hunger for little else.

AUDIENCE PARTICIPATION

A kid of eighteen, he had a prize-winning dick.
It glowed in the spotlight as he knelt to take
his partner in his mouth. Patiently, he'd endured
the other's sucking, it was part of the show,
but as they switched places, it was obvious the kid
preferred to do the sucking himself.

I stood close to the platform stage. A minuscule
mirrored ball and a glitzy curtain hung behind
the performing pair. The kid eyed me over the blowjob
and past the glare. Suddenly, he reached out, pulled me
up on the platform and down on my knees beside him.

We licked, we sucked, lubricating each other's mouths
as we ran our tongues along his partner's erect,
illuminated shaft.

When the other came, reaching down and clutching
the kid's shoulder, the boy threw his head back.
Chin glistening with cum, the kid's face, transformed
by ecstasy and lust, was as frenzied as a strangler's.

STOLEN THUNDER

Whatever sort of vehicle was parked alongside the bar,
van, Volkswagen, or limo, George the Faggot enthroned himself
and was offended, would correct you, if you didn't
refer to him the same way.

You'd see him there, in a lacy blouse, a tattered skirt,
always grimy. If he recognized you as someone who
strolled there often, he would smile and greet you.
But if you didn't use his title, "George the Faggot,"
when you returned his hello, he would correct you sternly.

New guys in town were shocked, startled or amused.
But natives came to recognize George as a landmark.
There was worried talk if no one saw him for a couple
of weeks. He lived on the streets, slept in the trucks
parked along the waterfront. No one could take him in.
Like an alley cat, scrappy and rangy, he scorned
a domestic lifestyle.

"They stole our thunder," George would say, "and I
stole it back again. Names are magic, names have power.
They took our name 'faggot' and used it against us.
They used our own power against us. So call me
'George the Faggot'! My power is in my name.
When someone calls me by my title, I hear thunder
over Manhattan and I feel the streets shake."

Everyone's worried. George hasn't been seen in a month.
Not even on West Street where he often turned tricks.
Just this morning, off the pier at the end of Christopher,
they hauled a young man's body out of the Hudson.
It wasn't George though.

6 BOYS 5 TIMES A DAY

Each boy danced clothed to a disco number,
the lights faded, came back up. Each boy stripped
to another disco number.

Indifferent to the proceedings, they danced limply,
gave little to the crowd, were cool, distant, smooth
as Hummel figures, contained, self-centered marionettes.

Boy #1 kept placing his palm against the fine
circle of hair around his navel. Boy #2 twiddled
his own nickel-sized tits. Boy #3's diamond pinkie-ring
glittered in time with the strobe. Boy #4 wore
a designer suit, sucked in his cheeks as he elegantly
disrobed. Boy #5 had an appendectomy scar.
Boy #6 was Jon.

He was not smooth. Furrows of hair lightly shaded
the contours of his ribs and thighs. Hair shaved close,
he wasn't coiffed. Jon wasn't cool. He looked deep into
the eyes of his watchers, teased them into trying to touch
him, let himself grow half-hard a foot from their faces,
let them imagine the vulnerable firmness of his balls,
feel his body heat as he moved his ass to the music.

He was doing it for the money and he loved it. One
of these old guys would surely have him first, but I
was still glad he'd be coming home to me.

WHAT LARRY SAID

Behind me the river, slothful with icebergs,
moved toward the harbor. Peter's down-jacketed back
receded farther and farther from me, and for the last time.
At least he chose a picturesque area in which to say
goodbye.

All I could think of was a story my friend Larry had once
told me. His father, after surgery, had to remain
in the hospital for several days. Larry quoted his mother
saying, "It broke my heart to have to leave your father
alone in that room. I wanted to get into bed with him and
stay, too." Larry expressed sorrow that there'd never be,
he was sure, anyone who would feel that way about him.

At the time I hadn't been moved. Acting the tough loner,
I remember saying, "Gays have to be prepared for tentative
relationships," implying it was bad manners for Larry
to reveal his lonely side.

But, watching Peter's back disappearing around the corner
and turning toward the slow progress of the cobalt water,
I considered what Larry said, unrepressed the vision
of myself 'old and alone,' consigned to a room as sterile
and vacuous as my need.

OBSCURE LODGINGS NEARBY

So California in his white clothes, sun-bleached hair
and moderate tan. So different from the other men
cruising the aisles of the Adonis.

Their eyes all looked inward. Wearing dark clothes,
they merged with the shadows. His eyes were wide.
I could see he was nervous when I stopped not far
from him.

He inched toward me along the short back wall behind
the seats. We smiled and quietly exchanged names.
He invited me to the Ramada Inn, two blocks down
Eighth Avenue.

Outside, the January air penetrated my leather jacket,
but he let his thin parka flap open in the wind.

His large room was orange and chocolate brown
instead of the expected orange and aqua.

He had almost as much light hair all over his body
as a lion-boy in a circus. His cock was as smooth
and curved as a tusk.

He cried like a child after he spent all over my chest,
his tears mixing with his semen.

He began to talk. I could see he needed to and I
let him. He was from San Diego. He worked in a bank.
He'd recently been married. He'd really loved his wife
at first...

MALE RAIN

I didn't go home this Christmas. After dinner,
he and I watched a National Geographic special.
The little blue lights from our improv tree
glinted in miniature on the television screen.

His parents had disowned him. They couldn't come
to terms with his conscientious objector status
or his homosexuality. And he was naturally reluctant
to meet my family. So I didn't go home this Christmas,
I stayed with him.

We'd had champagne in the bathtub, opened a present
each, gone for a refreshing walk by the river,
made love and had a long nap. But a shadow of depression
never left the edges of his eyes. And, since it was
my first Christmas away from home, I never did feel
quite right all day.

The National Geographic special was about an obscure
and dying African tribe. A woman with tattooed cheeks
stood in the rain and raised her arms, densely wound
with feather bracelets, toward the sky. She said,
"This is male rain. Female rain comes slowly, steadily,
fills the rivers and gives things life. Male rain
falls fast and bitterly like this, washes things away,
breaks trees, destroys."

The televised African woman went on, but he turned to me
and said, "Her knowledge must have been passed down
for generations. Will it take that much longer for us
to realize our capacity for filling the rivers,
for giving life? How long will it be before my family
understands me as a man with no wish to wash things away
or destroy?"

BABY JESUS COMES THROUGH FOR EASTER

for T.D.

It's a week since, in each other's arms, he said,
"For 2 and 1/2 years I've wanted to sleep with you,"
and I'd felt the same, seeing him at parties
or poetry readings, often accompanied by his lover.

But Holy Saturday night his lover was at work,
and though they spoke three times by phone while
I was there, I was not disappointed.

Not even when he asked, "Do you go to church?"
"Church," I joked, "it's redundant to go to church
on Easter. You should only go on off days.
Keeps Baby Jesus on his toes."

He seemed divided, wincing at the term 'Baby Jesus,'
but smiling too, murmuring "I'm very religious."

Buttoning my shirt, I noticed a cock-ring lying
under a chair, one with leather straps for encircling
the balls. "If I'd known it was so close by,
I'd have made you wear it."

He sat on the edge of the bed and pulled me to him,
pushing down my jockey shorts, sucking me into his
mouth. We had differences and his lover would later
be home, but for then he fondled, touched and held me
until I came. It was "as though a bridge were suddenly
erected across the impassable gulf," a phrase he
underlined in the book of poems he gave me.

INVOCATION AGAINST HOMOPHOBIA

As I was walking to the park I saw a man I thought
I recognized coming toward me. When he got closer
I realized I was mistaken. We were six feet apart
when he looked me straight in the eyes and spat
at my feet. "Faggot!" he hissed as I stepped over
the mess.

My hands contracted into fists and they shook.
I wondered at this since it was hardly my first
encounter with vehement homophobia. My shoulders
had tensed, raised instinctively against the seemingly
inevitable, but surprise attack.

Over the year, realizing the destructive force
of my own fierce resentments, I'd devised a prayer
to disarm my inner violence.

"My life is one with the unlimited life and power
of the cosmos. Its constructive power is within me,
building my mind and body into strength and perfection,
opening me to the health and peace of all things.
Positive vitality is flowing into every faculty and organ
of my being. I surround myself with a circle of light,
not only to shield me, but so that all who recognize it
or encounter it will be drawn to the unity of the cosmos
and healed."

Finished, still shaking with fury, not so much
at one silly man, but at all the times I'd ever flinched
because of my sexuality, the inescapable possibility
of abuse and violence which followed me everywhere,
I realized no prayer was going to cool this anger,
and surprising myself, I involuntarily screamed,
"I'll kill him!"

But the man, fortunately, didn't challenge me.
I sagged onto the steps of a brownstone and took deep
breaths, resting my head against the cool surface.

And later, returning from the park, I saw the same man
approaching again. "Oh, no," I thought and looked down
at the sidewalk, considering crossing the street
to avoid him. But then I thought, "Fate can't be avoided"
and I looked up again. He saw me. He, too, considered.

Suddenly, he cut between two parked cars and headed for
the opposite sidewalk, accelerating his stride.

JAMES DEAN TO ME

He stood near the turnstiles, a window into the back room
of the bookstore dark behind his head. He was the cashier
and bouncer. Humpy, but real straight. Though he
loved it when the boys checked him out.

His hair was light, lush and hardly combed. His nose
was constructed of quick angles. His full mouth
was chapped from the nibbles he kept nervously giving it.

He stood, legs apart, one hand in his pocket, stretching
the blue fabric tighter against the outline of his wallet,
his cock prominent as a roll of silver dollars.

He was the image of my hero, James Dean. Even his
pullover, dark red and faded, was right out of
Rebel Without a Cause.

I hid behind the black curtain, beneath the 'exit' sign
and let my eyes lick his thick crotch across twenty feet
and through his corduroy pants. I slowly caressed myself.

In my mind, I tasted his balls, tongued his fleshy buns,
bit his uptight lips until they bled.

He was straight and he was as wasted as the seed I shot.
He was just a low-class punk with a shit job, but right then
he was James Dean to me.

ANTHONY DIPIETRO

POEMS FOR BRYAN AND NO ONE ELSE

ANTHONY DIPIETRO IS A GAY SEX POET AND ARTS ADMINISTRATOR ORIGINALLY FROM PROVIDENCE, RHODE ISLAND. A GRADUATE OF BROWN UNIVERSITY WITH HONORS IN CREATIVE WRITING, HE ALSO EARNED A CREATIVE WRITING MFA AT STONY BROOK UNIVERSITY. NOW SERVING AS DEPUTY DIRECTOR OF THE ROSE ART MUSEUM AT BRANDEIS UNIVERSITY, HE RESIDES IN WORCESTER, MASSACHUSETTS. HE HAS A CHAPBOOK, *AND WALK THROUGH* **(SEVEN KITCHENS PRESS, 2021), AND HIS DEBUT COLLECTION,** *KISS & RELEASE* **(UNSOLICITED PRESS, 2024), WAS LONGLISTED FOR A MASS BOOK AWARD IN POETRY.**

WWW.ANTHONYWRITER.COM

INSTAGRAM @ANT.PROVIDENCE

AN ODE TO US

The #1 cure for writer's block is to visit
Rock River, a sacred few protected acres

in Vermont. Do you know a more poignant way
to say it is one of the last gay places?

The hike from the highway crosses the river,
demanding two kinds of footwear. A trail sign

marks boundaries: *FAMILY AREA CLOTHING PLEASE*—
'family' in this context means 'not gay.'

If you lose your pack or keys here, they will be
returned if you decipher codes we learned

before cell phones: handmade signs, invented
vectors, queer coordinates. When you reach

that curve of beach, ask the man with the watering can
if these garden flowers are his plantings.

'No, but I could see they needed it.'
On terraced trails above, nude men lean or drop low

to do what feels best in shade's hot press.
If you see two teen boys stride out, they may

greet you. The first in an affected
higher register says, 'Hey there,' & you, oblivious,

butch down your tone, 'Hello.' His friend jibes, 'No
thanks, I don't like dick'—which in this context means

he is one. A tiny joke. Maybe the most creative way
you've ever been called 'faggot' by dudes cruising by.

POEMS FOR BRYAN AND NO ONE ELSE

Prologue

While I walked to where I'm writing
this, a man met my eye on the sidewalk
and asked me to go with him to church
on Sunday. In any given assembly,
you can bet I will be best
at saying no. And sometimes also yes.

Ever Been to Battery 104 at Night?

Ahead you smell the ocean,

walk across a gravel field from dim
orange into total darkness, but you know
to turn in a few paces, left, where the paved path
rises that will bring you to him.

You left your car on Swallow Cave Road
by the walled estate where he summoned you
two nights ago. You found the entrance open, him
inside the screen, kneeling in a black

half-inch of fabric. When, friend, did you learn
how Boy possesses first and last control?
He brought you upstairs to the nursery
where his nanny raised him. He lay back, his

neck crooked, crammed in one corner
of a moonlit built-in window seat.
He gritted his teeth, but breathed, 'No, don't
you stop.' At the path's crown now, nothing

in your vision but constellations
rearranging. He leads you toward
the silent black tide, past the sign you know
reads *DANGER—CLIFFS UNSTABLE*,

to the broken cannon fortress,
stone foundations older than this country
rising from the rocks. You perch
together on a wide, cracked ledge,

& do as he asks. His butt and back
are dug in grit, your shorts dangle
from one sneaker in a shadow's
shadow, you kiss & penetrate & let him

film whatever the camera's eye can catch.

Interlude

I witnessed another man, either
blood hungry or painfully tired, hover
and stare at a fruit stand's abundance
of round reds, oblong yellows,
orange and green spilling over
edges of stacked wooden crates.

You Know the Type

Your new roommate covets
your many friends, so to get on your good side,
he introduces you to two
guys at the bar he sort of knows—

one exactly your type, from the length of his
scruff to the depth of his
dimples. His eyes lock in with yours,
so you dare him

to say your name twice & promptly
forget the other guy's name
& your roommate's. 'We're having
a party next weekend,' you shout,

'Let me put my number in your phone'
so you won't need to wait to start
text-flirting this very second, undetected
by the roommate & random guys

who order beer. He is typing
your name repeatedly, loudly, & you
are replying, soon everyone
whose name you don't know in the bar

is aware of the need
that magnets you both—I mean,
even the bartender feels
the gravitational pull—

& when he follows & closes the thin door
& removes his boots in your bedroom,
you find that he plays
like a man whose boyfriend

never lets him outside. Plays
like a saxophone solo that never leaves
the radio, & when you ask him
what he's never done,

he rubs his hair against your belly
& his answer gives you both big grins
like separated twins. There's no one in the city
doesn't know what you're up to tonight:

the sleep of scavenging animals
disordered by your dual howl. Oh, buddy—
the roommate story ends so badly. Maybe
you deserve it later, when he breaks

a window to make you believe
a burglar stole your TV—but listen,
you aren't the type of person
who regrets that which you choose.

My Song of the South

Call this one 'Shenandoah,'
translation: 'gay men living well on the mountain.'

You are cordially invited, Saturday noon,
the precise Height of Summer,

to a naked pool party,
where the duty to disrobe first

is entrusted to you & an artist from LA.
Enter he, all muscle & scar tissue,

open-mouthed, big-headed,
you instantly read his alpha energy,

you pull each other's skimpy
suits off, dive in, swim to one another,

full-body embrace against the pool wall,
& kiss in all four corners.

No soul has a view of the growing naked
fraternity, except chickens in their coop,

so you show the men how good is this
bounty of sunlit air, the pool's cool gleam,

scent of Callery pear. Who will wish
to follow you to the sauna with its wood

smell & an opera of men sighing? Or
is that sound wet drops dying

in the red hot heap of sauna stones?
A few come with you to the rental unit,

renovated antique trailer, mid-century modern
door open while you lie back on a shelf

& the invited artist eats your heartwood.
This wetness drying on warm skin.

There is no shape you beg for that he
can not create. No want unsatisfied.

No monument exists of metal, water,
wood, or stone. No monument but this.

Summer of a Dying Song

That was the summer of 'I can't feel
my face when I'm with you.' Truth is king
& throws his own heat: this is the summer
of dead flies & a threesome
like an origin story. You keep writing
but can only write to friends
saying, 'This is what my dying
feels like. How does your dying feel?'

The summer of 'Oh no, I've said too much,'
you were sexually awake to no one
but the muscular, bangled boy
in the music video who looks away
again & again.
                    Remember the primal cry:
summer of 'If you, if you could return,'
summer of 'Whispers at the bus stop,
nighttime in the schoolyard,'
summer of 'I alone tempt you,'
summer of 'Me & Cinderella,
we can drive it home with one headlight'—

Until summer of 'I want something else'
& sunrise at Scarborough Beach, you were lost,
admit it. Warrior wounded, lying awake in your tent
in the yard, the space you created for yourself.
Friend, do you believe
we each create such space?

The Objective Correlative of Shame

How dry his lips—skin peeling,
the mouth that begs
you to stand by his bed in blind dark
as he swigs from a square vodka bottle,
compels your hand to his opening, hounding,
'Come on, come on,' his hand pushing,
moving your fingers in & out.
He must have extra hands of his own.
To cry like that & never put the bottle down.

Rough

Nevermind the governor's aide who favors
hitting, his own eyes surprised
as he forces you to fight
for center & defend it, & you give
a good fight—

Forget the last-call hookup
straight from central casting (white tee,
black jeans, you half expected he'll run
a comb through his thick hair) who slaps &
razor burns your face red. When you can't
finish, he grumbles about how women
long ago, & now men bristle
at his ungentle forms of pleasure.

Tell instead about the Greek hairdresser,
third date at your loft, red wine, horror month,
his DVD collection, how he's disappointed
that vampire series aren't your jam.
The bottle empty before you sip.
Only then he remembers his Rx
mustn't mix with alcohol.

Sometimes you have to save
such scenes. Give up your bed,
crumple on your too-short couch,
stare up at the dark beams & wonder
where your karma went astray.

At first he sleepwalks to the bolted door,
where you meet him, confused,
turn him toward the bathroom,
help him find the bed again, tuck in.

Then the sound of your books & photos
flying from the shelf by your bed.
You switch on the light, climb the steps,
approach gently with his name
& a question mark. He cowers
& shakes in one corner, hands up

          to block his face, frightened eyes
through splayed fingers, in full fear
          looking up at you
like a father.

Twenty

You like his silver hair. Gary
works with you in Payroll, both temps who started
around the same time. You're twenty,
Gary maybe fifty. Has a 'roommate'
in Hillcrest & drives a white
classic Cadillac convertible. Gary says,
'Some of us are meeting
for drinks on Friday, want to join?'
You like his dimples, say 'Sure.' 'You want
a ride?' You like
his smile. You sit
on barstools facing
each other. You let him order
for you. He makes a show
of looking around, but there's no one else
coming from work. You like
his blue eyes. 'Well, you want to see
my condo? Meet my boyfriend?
Twenty-five years. Many cities.' You like
his martinis. His kindness. His
boyfriend, a masseur. 'He's certified,
he could give you a massage.
Right now, in fact, if you like.
His table's right in the next room. We have
towels.' No need, for you like being
in your underwear. You like having
your muscles handled
by the older men. How they look
at you. You like the massage table, the rubbing
of two against you. You like
the bedroom, the mattress. Like
lube & rubber cock rings & metal
& Gary's piercings. Gary's boyfriend.
Gary. His boyfriend. You do like
this life you are suddenly living.

Love Poem with Balcony

How do you write the love poem
for the man you met in 2019
whose name you still don't know
because, for years, he isn't real—

exists only in the night light, the space
where your two bodies invade
each other, thrilling the id to fullness with
getting what you want as soon as

you want it, where & how you like it.
He's known as Demon Boy. When you watch
How to Get Away with Murder,
he's Connor Walsh, wet-eyed villain you want

to apologize to. When you watch *Buffy*,
Demon Boy is Angel, brooding brow,
unknowable 275-year-old soul.
I forgot to say that you both say

'I love you'—that you love each other,
though some of your years
are drought years, or his silence is a forest
fire. You could not locate him

in a national emergency, but he has
bedded you in the boyfriend bed.
His apartment has a balcony where
you want to read the novel *Less* aloud to him

at sunset & tell him he's your Freddy Pelu.
Instead you climb in through the window
to the room where amyl nitrates remind you
how well you serve each other's

shadow-selves. Ask him again to show
you all his awful powers. Wait seven years
to start writing. Demon Boy knows he is Freddy, or
his silence insists that he knows.

Shame Revisited

It's not the years when you're sleeping
with both husbands, which is supposed to be
a secret, but the OK kind—

& it is not the way your heart races,
undressing at your locker, twisting the towel
around your waist at your first bathhouse—

it's the night you meet Henry's
twin brother, who's kind to you
in the same way that Henry is kind

because he remains in love with you
even though he has excised you.

You're alone with his twin
in Birmingham, drunk from much talk,

& in the cab, confused about where
you are moving. The twin shakes
his head & points toward his house.

He wants to invite you inside, you
understand, & go

so quiet that whole ride, trying to think
your way out of the black tar murk

inside you where you know
you will say yes to disaster

when he finally leans in & asks
or else takes. The car stops, he goodnights,

nothing happens. It isn't that, it is knowing
it would take nothing, half

a breath, for you to cross that threshold.

Epilogue

As I recall, Anne Carson wrote
something like, 'I'm not ashamed to say
I married him for beauty.'

Thank my stars, the guy I met
on 125th had a face that only a mother
or the God of Love could love.

JACK DRAGO
PRINCE OF THE GUTTER

JACK DRAGO IS A CREATOR OF EXPERIENCES, A GUIDE INTO REALMS WHERE THE SENSUAL AND THE SPIRITUAL INTERTWINE. HE BELIEVES IN THE SACREDNESS OF SEX AND IN THE POWER OF RITUAL—KNOWING THAT ANYTHING, APPROACHED WITH THE RIGHT MINDSET, CAN BECOME A PORTAL TO TRANSFORMATION. HE WRITES WITH HEAT, SHADOW, AND NERVE. HIS POETRY IS A DARK CARNIVAL OF LUST, DEFIANCE, AND SELF-REVELATION THAT STRIPS AWAY PRETENSE AND MOVES FROM SURREAL INVOCATION AND APOCALYPTIC VISION TO MOMENTS OF INTIMATE FEROCITY. HE SPLITS HIS TIME BETWEEN LAS VEGAS AND BERKELEY, WHERE HE WORKS ALONGSIDE THE LEGENDARY BOB KURTZ CO-CURATING *COLLECTORS REALM 3,* **THE DIGITAL EVOLUTION OF THE ICONIC BERKELEY STOREFRONT, ONCE A VIBRANT HUB WHERE PUNK CULTURE, QUEER HISTORY, AND VINTAGE EROTIC ART COLLIDED. SINCE THE SHOP'S CLOSURE IN 2014, DRAGO AND KURTZ HAVE KEPT ITS SPIRIT ALIVE ONLINE, BUILDING A LIVING ARCHIVE OF VINTAGE GAY PHOTOGRAPHY AND AVANT-GARDE ART THAT PRESERVES THE RAW, UNAPOLOGETIC ENERGY OF ITS ORIGINS. WWW.COLLECTORSREALM3.NET**

BLEEPITY BLOPPITY BLOOP

They say what AI can bring
What Mankind has dreamed, so
Bleepity bloppity bloop

Put 'em together and what have you got?
Bleepity bloppity bloop

Train up a matrix,
Adjust your weightings
Bleppity bloppity bloop

It'll do magic, believe it or not!
Bleepity bloppity bloop

Now singularity means
That the AI will always improve
So if it's not good enough
To steal your job then
Bleepity bloppity bloop

Train up a matrix,
Adjust your weightings
Bleppity bloppity bloop

Adversarial networks
Detect all the flaws and
Bleepity bloppity bloop

Now nobody's job is safe
And computers can self-improve
The thingamob has taken your job
And the age of work is through!

Robots are coming,
Hit the ground running
Bleepity bloppity bloop

You'll never outrun them
No matter the cost
Bleepity bloppity bloop

HAIL ASEMODEUS

Hail Asemodeus, patron of heat,
breaker of wedding bands,
king of the tables where dice fall
like the souls of men.
I have felt you breathing in my marrow,
long before I knew your name.
Was it you who made me a beacon,
irresistible to eyes that could not love,
only consume?
Johnny's ghost walks inside me still,
sweet child, paper skeletons pinned to the wall,
a mind dreaming of medicine,
a heart dreaming of his mother.
Until the door opened,
and the shadow blotted out the hall-light,
and innocence was not lost but taken,
throttled into silence.
A small boy learned
the world is no safe place to live in,
so he went away.
And I came.

I came with no childhood to speak of,
only highlights,
like postcards from a stranger's vacation.
Expo '86.
The Challenger's falling fire.
Bits of a life,
stitched over the hollow where a boy once was.

You used me well, great demon.
Moonlit streets, middle school streaking,
bodies met in whispers and parked cars,
older hands teaching away innocence.
I learned to offer myself like incense.
I learned to hunger.
Through motels and beaches,
through smoke-filled rooms where men
slammed veins
and chanted in your honor,

through acts so far past shame
that shame became a rumor,
I was your acolyte.
Flesh was my scripture,
pain my confirmation,
drugs the censer that kept the altar sweet.

I have been goat and boy,
slave and prince of the gutter.
I have been an open door for every Beast,
and each one left a mark
I still trace with trembling fingers.

Asemodeus,
you were there in the first gasp,
you will be there in the last.
You gave me the body as a weapon,
the heart as a stake to be driven through,
and I, obedient child,
have bled you a lifetime of offerings.

SWEET JESUS, AL PARKER!

What if I took away
Your picture of Jesus
Replaced it with the portrait
Of the porn star Al Parker?

Would you pray to Al Parker,
Beg him for your salvation,
Like so many others had begged
For an orgasm from his cock?

Perhaps God found it a moral
Improvement on Cesare Borge.

[At this point the poet talked
The priest he was corrupting
Into working a picture of
Al Parker into a PowerPoint
With a Jesus quote.]

MUSCLE

Gotta get strong, gotta get big muscles, boys like big muscles, gotta get strong, lift weights every day to get strong, one more rep, one more rep to get strong; doesn't count unless it hurts, doesn't count unless you're too tired to move when you're done, get strong, lift weights every day, big muscles, boys like big muscles, one more rep and make it count, lift 'em slow, stretch when you're done, big muscles and tight abs, I feel flabby when I miss a day, tighten those abs, work out every day, the weights are light, gotta add more weight, add more weight for big muscles, feels good to work out, make it count, doesn't count unless you're too tired to move when you're done, stretch when you're done and make it good, gotta get big, gotta get strong, wanna look like the boys in the magazines, big muscles, tight abs, hard pecs, work out every day and look like the boy in the magazine, work those muscles hard, gotta make every rep count, make 'em strong, one more rep, one more rep to make 'em strong, make your muscles big and strong, one more rep nice 'n slow, make it count, make every motion count, work out every day, heavy weights for a hard body, work your muscles hard, doesn't count unless it hurts, doesn't count 'till every muscle is tired, get big muscles, boys like big muscles, lift weights every day and be strong, gotta get strong, big and strong, work out every day to be big and hard and strong, gotta get strong, want big muscles like you wanna get high, the weights are light, add more weight, add more weight to make your muscles hard, wanna be big and hard, feels good to work out, feels good to lift weights, weights make you strong, gotta get strong, look like the boy in the magazine, big muscles, boys like big muscles, gotta lift every day to get big muscles, miss a day and you feel weak, miss a day and you feel flabby, gotta work the weight every day, get strong, big and strong, make every muscle bulge 'till your body is perfect, work every muscle 'till you're too tired to move, one more rep and make it count, doesn't count unless you're too tired to move; gotta get strong, do more reps for bigger muscles, one more rep for stronger muscles, your body

OBSESSION

is puny, gotta build muscle every day or you feel small, gotta work hard, feels good to work hard, make every rep count, doesn't count unless it hurts, stretch when you're done, big muscles, boys like big muscles, lots of reps for big muscles, gotta get big, big and strong, gonna lift weights every day 'till every last muscle is a big ass bulge, gonna do one more rep to make sure I'm stronger, gotta get stronger, gotta get bigger 'cuz bigger is better, big arms, big legs, tight belly, lift weights to get bigger, gotta work out every day, stretch when I'm done, feels good to lift weights, feels good to be strong, one more rep, just one more rep to get strong, the weight is light, wanna work harder, get bigger 'cuz bigger is better, one more rep and make it count, doesn't count unless it hurts, gotta work 'till it hurts a little, gotta make yourself do just one more, feels good to lift hard, stretch when you're done, miss a day and you feel flabby, gonna work out every day, gonna do just one more rep, your body is puny, gotta stretch, gotta work harder, gotta do one more rep, yeah, one more rep, nice and slow, one more rep to get strong, big and strong, big and strong and hard with every muscle bulging, gotta get big, boys like big muscles, feels good to lift weights, feels good to stretch, feels good to lift hard, feels good to make it count, miss a day and you feel weak, gotta work every day, stretch when I'm done, get strong, gotta get strong, gotta get big, just one more rep for bigger muscles, feels good to work hard, gonna work out every day, make every muscle bulge 'till my body is perfect, boys like perfect bods, gotta work every muscle 'till I'm too tired to move, gotta get strong, big and strong 'cuz bigger is better, big muscles and tight abs, I wanna look like the boy in the muscle magazine, wanna lift weights like I wanna do drugs, one more rep to make sure I'm stronger, one more rep and make sure it counts, gotta get bigger 'cuz bigger is better, big arms, big legs, tight abs, hard pecs, lift weights every day for the perfect body, boys like perfect bodies, gotta get strong, work hard every day, big, bulging muscles, and stretch when I'm done, stretch when I'm done.

WE ARE THE UNIVERSE TRYING TO UNDERSTAND ITSELF

We are the Universe
trying to understand itself—
the miracle of consciousness:
incredibly improbable,
yet absolutely inevitable,
given the laws of nature,
enough space, and enough time.

Think of the forces needed
to shape the vast country inside...
your mind is the legacy
of every interaction of every ancestor
all the way up your line.
Shaped by every circumstance in history
to be exactly what they are,
to fit their place in the grander scheme,
and to help each and every one of us survive.

Riding the wave of the eternal now,
on and on down the river of time,
through an endless succession of survivors
stretching all the way back
to the origin of life—
trying an infinite diversity
in infinite combinations,
endlessly branching,
diverging and combining,
trying every possible solution,
keeping only what works.

And now, we have discovered
this process for ourselves:
testing our ideas against the Universe,
conforming them unto its will.

We go on collecting knowledge
as we strive for understanding,
and survive into the future,
letting it mold the generations—
until we can reach our mother, the stars.

We are all made of star stuff,
exploded out across the eons
and endlessly recycled—
right back to the beginning of time.
What magic could be required
for this to be any grander?
And there is no shame here
if we do not yet understand it.
That's okay.
It's what we're here for—
and we're doing the best we can.

REVOLVING DOOR SATANIST

You stared into the void,
then ran in terror.
I don't blame you.
Fear is a perfectly valid response.
Some meet it with fascination,
some with dread,
some with both in the same breath.
However you feel about it is fine.
Many before you have felt the same.
Ours is not a faith of locked gates.
No marble staircase to crawl in penance,
no bloodied knees for forgiveness.
The devil prefers a revolving door,
a reminder that you are always free
to come and go as you wish.

O, inconstant one,
if you only knew the cycles I've endured.
If my power terrifies you,
I make no apology.
It is an accurate perception,
perhaps the first truly accurate one
you have ever had.
You have the right to decide
whether a demon in human form
is worthy of such power.
As for me,
the devil entrusted me with it,
and that is enough for my purposes,
though I understand if it's not for yours.
I told you I'd let you run in circles
as long as you needed
to burn through your fear.
I will keep that promise.
I respect your right to
open your soul like a flower,
let the devil in all night,
then wear your suit and tie to work
with that secret still warm inside you.

I respect your right to run from it,
and your right to seek it
like a moth to flame.
All are valid experiences,
vital to spiritual maturation.
This is the left-hand path:
to face our shadows
and make them into strength.
The void within you is yours alone.
Feel what you feel,
but give yourself the space
to know that in time,
you might feel differently.

I WANT YOUR ASS

I can't stop thinking about ass. Man ass.
Thick and juicy boy booty, and
I'm gonna nut inside your butt,
Because raw is law, or not at all.
I wanna see your ass.
Yeah, show me that ass.
I like your ass. Can I touch your ass?
I wanna feel that beautiful butt.
I wanna smell behind your balls,
Lemme lick your ass.
I wanna taste your hole.
Put my tongue inside,
And make you moan.
Your ass is delicious.
I could eat it all day,
But my cock is hard
And there's a better way.

Can I stick it in?
Maybe just the tip?
Is it nice and tight?
Or can I let 'er rip?
I wanna fuck your ass.
I wanna breed you raw.
I wanna plant my seed
In your gaping maw.

Lemme fuck your ass. Balls deep.
Buried to the hilt is how I breed.
I ain't gonna be gentle
When I get in my rut,
Cuz I gotta be brutal if I want to nut.
Gonna pound dat ass 'till it's destroyed.
Lemme wreck your hole
And make it leak my slime.

OUTLINE OF EVIL

```
    /-- HELL ----\ /--------------====DEMON
pervrt /-    |   ||     /-power__/        \
  |_filth    | /-control--\ |          promisc
  | ||   /-captivity |   service      /  |
 PIG_/+=tempt     |  |      >surrender---ass
     |  | \\   | _|  __humil   |
      \ |    PAIN--maso/      \ |
      sacrifice-\|     |     __soulsuck
        \       | /-bodyart /
         \      CBT     | /
       blood--\ | /--mutil     |
asphyx-\  |    /-castr
       snuff
```

WAYSTATION OF THE DAMNED

Somewhere on the edge of civilization
lies the last gas for 800 miles.
Somewhere on the edge of the
vast and inhospitable desert,
near the base of a dark and
imposing mountain, can be found
the Waystation of the Damned.

You look up above the apron,
at the burned-out, vinyl-wrapped sign:
a SHELL sign, with the first letter
both burned out and missing, as if
taken out by a stray bolt of lightning
from the ominous gray clouds behind
that iron-rich Battle Mountain—
landmark of the battle-born state.

Gas, maps, and snacks inside,
providing service with a smile,
always going the extra mile
to make sure that every customer
gets exactly the things he needs—
whether that's advice or directions,
or a quick fumble in the restroom
(which happens more often than
he would prefer to admit to you),
or even a hand-in-hand tour guide
all the way to your destination,
if that's what you need to make it.

Where are they going to wind up?
Will they finally make it there?
These questions are declared
"above my pay grade" by him,
the humble keeper of this place.

"Some people come around here,
and they stock up for the journey,
and they move on—
you never see 'em again.

Some people, they come ’round,
and they take one look at the desert,
and they wisely decide to turn back.
I never saw those much afterwards, neither.

And sometimes people choose to
come back and back again here.
That’s what I call good customers.
They’ll go out to the point of no return,
and be stoppin’ for gas on the way back.
Bless ’em, they’ll get there someday.”

We take all comers here at the waystation,
and we honor every customer’s right
to go exactly as far as they choose to,
and come back as many times as they
can afford to. It’s our calling, after all.

BACK COVER MAN

Well I'm your back cover man,
You don't know who I am.
Well if you want to know more
You could turn to page four
But that just ain't who I am.

Well I'm your back cover man,
And it ain't going to plan.
It would have filled me with joy
To be this month's cover boy
But that just ain't who I am.

I'm just your back cover man,
And I'm showing my tan.
I'll be putting on a show
Everywhere that you go,
But that's just magazines, man.

MATTIE FRYE

IT'S NOTHING PERSONAL

MATTIE FRYE IS A GRADUATE STUDENT IN THE REINHARDT UNIVERSITY CREATIVE WRITING MFA PROGRAM AND HAS WORKED FOR TWO YEARS ON THE EDITING TEAM FOR THE *JAMES DICKEY REVIEW*. **SHE IS A FORMER PUBLIC SCHOOL TEACHER AND WILDLIFE EDUCATOR WHO IS RAISING TWO CHILDREN WITH HER PARTNER. SHE LIVES AMONG THREE GENERATIONS OF FAMILY IN HER CHILDHOOD HOME IN NORTH GEORGIA.**

YOU AND ME WITH OUR CLOTHES ON

Today one of those Shriners standing by the highway off-ramp hit on me through my sunny, open window. It felt harmless. I responded with genuine amusement, and when he walked away, I surveyed his form. He had a certain type of lithe spareness found in some men over sixty. He looked a little like Leonard Cohen from *Popular Problems*. Not bad. A decade ago, I would have ashed my cigarette into his donation box—or at least wanted to. I learned to avoid spitting, legally it could be considered assault. With my friends I used to take my shirt off in the back seats of cars, a catharsis of moment and momentum. With my little sister I used to stare down men who would press their gaze into my sedan at red lights. Late at night I used to lean out of the window on I-75, screaming for the guy in the muscle car to show me his tits. For years I used to lay in my bed and comfort myself to sleep by repeating: I'll never have sex.

There was a sermon at church in which two members acted out the temptation of Jesus in the desert. The devil was played by a young, unmarried man who grew up in the church. He was a writer, and he looked a little like the kid from *Home Alone* but dressed like a typical sitcom dad. He could have been a weird, stoic third uncle in *Full House*. He had a sensitive face but only ever smiled in a wry, sarcastic kind of way. That morning he wore a black short-sleeved button up, black Levi's, and shiny black cowboy boots that echoed on the hardwood floor. When he was the devil he moved like liquid, draped himself across the pew, his voice unconcerned and a little bit playful. He did not menace or give commands. I liked him. I was 6 and I didn't pay much attention to the talking in church and usually just watched the wasps buzz around the slowly spinning ceiling fans. I remember hoping that him and Jesus could work it out and still be friends. I remember wishing that I could come alive like that one day too, smoothed out and confident. Mostly I remember wanting something. I do not remember who played Jesus.

Other people's attraction still felt like something someone strapped onto me, maybe it was armor or maybe it was a live explosive, but either way it slowed me down and made me easier to catch. I was 18 and the youngness in me overflowed and seemed to always belong to other people, ones with empty eyes and hands. What was a blank page to me was someone else's fatted calf. It was inconvenient. It was something else too. I was starting to learn to make myself sharp and weaponized, but it was tiring. I was waifish, but I had nice legs. My jeans were baggy, but I usually didn't wear a bra. My coat in the winter made me look like Kramer, but in the summer I was almost bare. There were only a few options spilled out on the table: Hello Kitty brass knuckles, a water gun full of tequila, a nice heavy rock. I vowed to love my body, its magic and myth. I let down my hair and was Morgan le Fey. Being a girl was still a minimum wage job I couldn't get fired from, but I was learning to slip out back for smoke breaks.

When I met you, you weren't wearing shoes. Your white shirt was mostly unbuttoned. You wore a pendant on a silver chain and a gold pinky ring. You were relaxed, almost dainty. Blithely, obstinately happy. Definitely high. You had a lot of hair. You were almost my height. There was a joint stuck behind your ear and you smiled at me prettily across the counter. You had a beauty mark right above your lip and faint nicotine stains on your front teeth. You asked after our manager and sometimes drug dealer. You asked what I was reading. I held up *Doors of Perception*. I was staring, telling myself it would be the last time, that next time I would be stronger. You promised to bring me *A Season in Hell* when you could find your copy. You were between homes right now, living in your friend's Camaro parked behind the movie theater. You breezed back down the dark hallway and outside in a square of blinding white. I stared after you for a long time, blinking away your after image.

My mother and I watched a lot of classic movies. I saw one with Humphrey Bogart once and couldn't look away from the scenes where he walked alone down a dimly lit street. In my room with the door closed I would practice that walk, wearing one of my father's winter coats. I was just a kid, and I did not have the words to say what I wanted. I knew I didn't want the obligation that came with beautiful. I wanted the anonymity that his suit gave him. The way he seemed to move free and without the disclaimer I saw pinned to the back of every gown on screen: Woman. I saw how they all walked in and immediately had to start proclaiming things. Humphrey Bogart walked on screen and just stood there, smoking. I hated him. He had something I knew belonged to me. I wanted to make those bright and shining women actually smile. I could be suave, or painfully earnest, or flash my white teeth at them and earn a swift slap to my cheek. I would like it.

My first boyfriend was jarringly, mistakenly smitten with me. I refused him several times and then asked him out myself. I took a Polaroid of his face when he read the personalized message in the fortune cookie and laughed at him as it developed. I was 16 and I loved him like a science fair experiment. I broke up with him three months later when he broke my rules and gave me flowers and a note that said "I love you" on Valentine's Day. My next boyfriend was a bad kisser, but we watched David Lynch movies together crammed on the recliner. He said amusing things like "the sexiest thing a guy can wear is jeans and no shirt," which I liked, and that I wasn't invited out with our friends because he needed "guy time," which I didn't. They were diverting and temporary. It was only a matter of time until I was relegated squarely to the side of Girlfriend in their minds, and then it was over. Before that I would feel the deep buried pleasure of having pulled one over on them, that I lured them in with the promise of girl and then delivered something else. I ignored the even deeper splinter of hope that they might like it.

When we had to start dressing out in P.E., my mother told me with gravity, as if delivering the news of someone's untimely death. It was clear to me that my mother had not taken well to public locker rooms in her day. She explained that I would have to change into my gym clothes, in front of my locker, in front of everyone else. I have never been bothered by my naked body. My older sister called me a nudist well into grade school. But my mother was painfully shy. When I heard the news my first thought was not that my peers would see me naked, but that I would see them. These thoughts were not yet fully formed and lay dormant under a thick, protective layer of ice. There was, however, a strong sense of self-preservation that beeped somewhere in the distance, like a smoke alarm needing its batteries changed. My mother took my silence as admission of my own embarrassment and vowed to buy me long camisoles I could wear, to keep me covered. I wondered which girls wouldn't be wearing them.

Before we got together, when you let me keep you in a careful orbit, I liked to give you jewelry. A pink and red carnelian anklet you wore until it snapped, spilling out into the grass. A round, gold pendant of St. Francis that I stole for you from the Basilica in Assisi. We lost that one too, in an empty dorm we broke into, after a party we weren't invited to, at a college we didn't attend. I started buying the cigarettes you liked. You took me to a pretty, green hill that was really a landfill they covered in grass. You let me fill my arms up with you, bear your weight while I bared my throat. I felt a little like Lancelot, a little like Puck. You were Rimbaud in the evenings, Joan of Arc when we woke up. A girl we worked with bummed a cigarette from me by the dumpster and tried to ask me about you. I couldn't remember if you fucked her or refused her, maybe it was both. Aren't you worried that he's… her lip lifted like it had been caught on a hook. Gay? I flicked my cigarette, and it landed in the next parking space over. I unsheathed my smile. Why do you think he likes me so much?

The first time someone thought I was a boy I was in 9th grade. I went with my friend to our inaugural high school Halloween party. I dressed up like a greaser, Ponyboy Curtis to be exact, but I knew better than to tell anyone that. I made a fake cigarette with Kool printed neatly on the side. I wrapped an ace bandage around every inch of my torso. I dusted my jaw and upper lip with the faintest eye shadow. I practiced my best Bogie smile in the mirror. When I got to my friend's house, she was wearing a pink fringed skirt and matching top. I was dimly aware that our differences in costumes might mean something, but it skittered away when reached for like whatever is always rolling around under the driver's seat. At the party we did not drink but acted like we had. The next day at school a boy we met sat down at the lunch table next to my friend, grinning at her, laughing about something that happened at the party. When I responded he gave me a look and insisted he didn't remember seeing me there. I said I was dressed like a greaser. Oh shit, I thought you were a dude! Much to my mortification, I blushed. He apologized with stumbling profusion, didn't bother getting my friend's number, and made a hasty retreat. I smiled stupidly at my food, face burning. I wasn't sure why I could hear my own heartbeat in my ears. I wasn't sure how to say that it was a compliment.

We were in the Taco Bell drive thru when my mom handed me my cheese quesadilla and asked, are you a lesbian? I knew why she would ask this. I had just given my 8th grade persuasive speech on marriage equality. Prop 8 was all over the news and she was getting tired of me talking about it, dramatic and unopposed from the passenger seat. I checked the bag for diablo sauce. No mother, I'm not a lesbian. I did like boys, their salt smell, the oddly delicate bones of their ankles, the soft strip of skin between their hair and their collar, the downy strands above their lips, on their earlobe, above their knees. It was easy to say no. Lesbian sounded like a door on which I needed to knock and be invited in. At school, when I was separated from my friends and sat drawing comics in the margins on my notes, boys looking to make a splash would often walk up to me, smiling over their shoulder at their friends within ear shot. Are you a lesbian? The words were aimed like a missile but shot through the air like a comically deflating balloon and dropped innocuously at my feet. If someone had asked if I liked girls, I would have said yes. I thought maybe everyone liked girls, at least a little. Why else were they so magnetic? I gave my patent answer, which at the time I thought was very clever. I don't know, are you?

My friends sometimes made jokes about me stealing their girlfriends. Only once was it a little bit true. It didn't occur to me until decades later that there might be words for that. At the end of each party, we would always find ourselves asleep on the floor together, my head tucked neatly under your chin. People were a little wary of us. They said we didn't seem like we were dating. They said we spent too much time together. They were a little jealous, a little frightened by the lack of space we left between us. At the vulnerability. The lack of definition. We brushed our teeth shoulder to shoulder, no His and Hers sinks. When people came to the apartment, they would be greeted by our benefactor and friend, who was both gregarious and unsettling, and looked like a stretched-out Clint Eastwood on acid. Then the camera would pan left to us, the talk show host's perpetual special guests, wearing each other's clothes with legs intertwined like a couple of Siamese cats. I painted your nails while you held a cigarette to my lips. People couldn't find the right insults to point out what they thought was wrong, but they would just sense it and start twitching like a bomb dog.

I'm pregnant with our son and polishing off another box of gluten free matzo crackers when my 7th period class starts trickling in. One of my students loiters at my desk, looking for snacks and some attention. She picks up a framed photo of me and you and our daughter from my desk and turns to me, asking how we were able to conceive. I am grateful for my mouthful of crackers. I take my time answering. Last time I checked this wasn't health class. She looks at me embarrassed and a little disappointed but aiming for indignant. Well, I thought you guys were—she gestures up and down at my body in the chair and I pull my usual card of levity. Why, because I'm wearing men's pants? She puts the photo back down. I just didn't know you were straight. She shrugs but continues to linger. I turn back to my computer, scanning through the PowerPoint for today's lesson. I smile. Yeah? I guess cause I'm not. People don't seem to mind us much anymore. We check a lot of boxes, we have the two kids, the straight white teeth, the framed, glossy photos. Another student asked me why I choose to go by Mrs. They seemed, a little bit, to pity me. I explained that I didn't think anyone could be forced into understanding. I knew what it felt like to have somebody understand and you can't cram all that into a pronoun. I explained that they could feel differently, that they could decide what those words could mean for them. Context is a noun, but it seems like it does a lot of moving. I can just lay there and let it slide things, fit things, arrange things all around me. I can let it do all the work.

IT'S SOMETHING SPECIAL, TO PAINT YOUR HOUSE GREEN

And let it slide a little further into the landscape, like it could belong there, or like it could take off with silent, indifferent wings one day, your headlights shining on an empty lot when you return from work that evening. People go crazy for painting a house white, everywhere I turn they've gone and painted another one. A white house can't slink off anywhere except in the snow. If you don't have snow, it has nowhere to escape. It just sits there glaring like the dry, bleached bones of a long dead animal. It's easy to point it out on the horizon. Exposed. It's easy for people to crawl inside.

I used to dream of living alone with a baby in a yellow, stucco house. The baby was mine, but I did not know where it came from. Every day we would paint, and no one would ever visit. I used to imagine living in a house with low stone walls around the garden and a marble altar. I would plant jonquils, lavender, marigolds, yarrow. A whole bed of foxgloves. Barberry beside the door. Hawthorne outside my bedroom window. I cried once to my mother because one day I would grow up and have to leave our home. She burned a little brighter when she told me no, I could stay here forever.

I am not a human girl, I would think. I knew that something was wrong before puberty, but when I turned 13 I learned the word "changeling." I looked at photos that showed me as a baby, a toddler, 5, 6, 7. I saw that she was not me. When I tried to pry the truth out of her soft, little eyes, there was only the coolness of perfect shade. I was certain that the girl in the photo would float if you laid her down in the quiet of the river. And I could feel the shape of it then, that cancerous howl, the thing I knew would send me sinking, plummeting beneath the surface.

The girl must have been outside on an early morning, maybe she didn't know it was Beltane, Midsommer, the last full moon before fall. She would have been the type of girl who ached for magic, who was always waiting for it to pierce through her, needle sharp. The sky would have looked waxy like it sometimes does, like you could dig your fingers into the colors, feel them under your fingernails. I don't think they would have hurt her, only basked in the round coins of her eyes, her honest, green captivation. They would have braided her hair and given her strong drink and woven their silver stories and songs until she fell asleep. And their only crime would have been forgetting her after.

In the darkness of my childhood bedroom, my body is the warm and familiar shape it takes when my children mold themselves to me in sleep. Across town in the sterile black of a storage facility sit the boxes meant to furnish my fabled family home, the one that has failed to materialize. Sets of cobalt blue drinking glasses. A round kitchen table. Legions of books. All packed away to make room for bins of diapers, blankets, so many tiny shoes. We breathe our singular breath, returning for a moment to the time where I am shelter enough. Asleep, their hands move to press into the soft clay of my skin, leaving behind handprints, indecipherable runes, just below my navel.

I know that she was not buried, she stayed resting there with her cheek against the velvet of moss. I do not like to think about her decomposition, the slow violence of time making ugly her pink skin, her downy curls. But I think often of her scoured bones, the little pearls of her teeth, unyielding and unafraid after so much sun and rain. I think of their stark gleam, the startling whiteness against the collage of rotting leaves, the purple blanket of wild phlox. I used to be certain which parts of my story were true, but not anymore. The house we come back to each evening is the gray of shifting smoke and heavy clouds, and when it swallows us we are home.

LIFE CYCLE OF A STAR

I was sitting splay legged on the toilet, body numb from a night of Old Crow and staring as I always did at the poster on the wall of a friend's bathroom. It was a photo from the Hubble space telescope revealing some points of light, swirls of gasses, and blackness. The white words at the top proclaimed it "The Life Cycle of a Star" and scattered across the poster were short paragraphs explaining the science behind all that. The one I was staring at in my private, timeless sabbatical, the only one I ever read, stated "young stars form together in clusters of sister stars." In the darkness and sudden quiet of the bathroom this always read as profound, a line drawn from the poster to my life in one easy arc, and yet it dissolved like sugar, a sticky perversion of what it once was, when I would return to the living room.

My partner was cross legged on the pull-out mattress, and despite the unreasonable hour was still wearing cheap black slacks peppered with cigarette burns and a woman's white button up shirt. I was still an interloper in this world, an amusing hanger-on to the owners of the apartment. They were attempting to lure their friend back into their lives more permanently, the way people leave out food for feral cats. Without me they couldn't get him through the door. But there is an endearment that comes through forced cohabitation, and it was catching. I settled back down while he was performing our night's required labor of rolling a half ounce worth of joints, and did so without his eyes leaving the screen. In my absence he turned on *Factory Girl.*

I watched the likeness of Edie Sedgwick from behind the silhouette of his profile, real and warm and alive beside me. The movie itself was a source of near constant bitching, but it was one of the few DVDs that has made it to this particular apartment and so each one had taken on an almost ritualistic role in our nights. He was constantly correcting the facts presented on screen, but he held a fondness for the film, a touchstone to something he both couldn't capture and couldn't outrun. He seemed to identify with all troubled, artistic, or ill-fated women, his chosen saints. He rattled off facts about them the way 10-year-old boys did with their baseball cards. The movie was a backdrop, an overlaying of a feeling and place we could smoke and laugh and bicker to. But I had seen him drunk, the first time he showed me this movie, and watched his wet eyes meet hers through the screen, and witnessed an eerily splintering pain spreading like a cracked windshield, the twin desire to find that pain a home.

I finished my cigarette and watched the pictures slide by. I thought of the photograph of her that I remember best, one where she is sitting cross legged on a pillow, face partially obscured by her hand bringing a cigarette to her lips. She is wearing a pink gown that looks all the more soft from her place on the floor. Her eyes are squinting in a possible smile and behind her there is a cord for the lamp, some bit of fabric wrinkled on the floor. Beside her foot is a little blue dish where she could ash her cigarette. There is something about the setting that draws me, an ordinary tone to the picture that becomes almost intimate.

At that time, we were always hunkering down in smoky apartments to watch movies like this, movies where you watch somebody get dragged down. I was afraid to speak it aloud, as if there existed no wood that could unknock it, that I was the only one who understood we were living in the first act of those stories. I was aware that everyone in the apartment could cram onto this filthy mattress and in the flicker of the TV would see themselves as Edie Sedgwick. Our heartbroken, meth dealing cowboy. His sociopathic little girlfriend who stole my gold paged tarot card book. My alcoholic, homeless sweetheart. Maybe even me, but I'm afraid I was more like Edie's friend, a person whose advice might make someone leap from a car and run madly into the street. There was a distance between Edie and Andy that they couldn't seem to jump, maybe what looked like a few inches to me was actually light years for them.

We were not in New York City. We were in a truck stop of a town where none of us even grew up. It offered privacy, but only because it possessed such a vacancy of spirit that it seemed to dissolve everything within it, like acid rain dissolves a tombstone. Mostly it was empty, cracked parking lots, carpet warehouses, and strip mall liquor stores. The apartment was a matchbox across the street from a train depot. We could be in our hometowns in twenty minutes. We could be in Midtown in an hour. We weren't stuck here, but we played disciples to all the beauty we couldn't touch by purging it. There was a burn and a bliss to watching New York on the screen, and a permission to toss it all back over your shoulder like garbage when you were done.

IT WAS NOT A HOUSE

It was a 1989 Volvo DL, but we slept there sometimes, intertwined and stiff-necked, on nights when nothing was in the works and no one was offering a couch. Sleeping in your car isn't always easy, it's mostly about killing time and avoiding cops. There was a good chance that if we stopped, the car wouldn't start again. We kept it moving. If the engine didn't turn over, I would smoke a ritual cigarette and try again. It almost always worked. If there was nothing planned, we would wait in places that we knew were safe. We parked outside a friend's house and sat on her porch. She got off at midnight, would join in for a smoke, then kick us out. Later, after she moved, we would still sit in the car outside her vacant house, the porch piled with unclaimed junk. They tore it down a few years later.

We could catch a few hours of sleep behind the movie theatre once the manager we didn't party with went home. We could stop for a while outside a Waffle House, as long as we bought something first, an All-Star breakfast, an egg biscuit with tomato, a dozen cups of burnt coffee. I kept a moving blanket on the backseat. In the summer we didn't need it. In the winter it wasn't enough. Most of the time something was happening. There was a friend looking for a ride to a kickback in Alabama. There was a futon in a basement. There was an empty bit of sky where the stars had been, and the sun soon would be.

DEAD PETUNIAS BY THE FRONT DOOR

I pulled into an empty driveway. I had been somewhere I hadn't said I'd be, but that was last night, and it was past noon now and the sun evaporated what was left of the gin and the guilt. I did not get out of the car. No one was home, and the front door was almost impossible to open, some problem with the deadbolt that required you to heave up and in with the handle while twisting the key.

Somehow, I was sobbing. I should have been relieved to have the house to myself. I could shower and change, unfurl myself slowly from my chosen chaos without any scrutiny. Maybe when my cards were shuffled, a day came loose and found itself here, inexplicable and strange. Maybe on the day I come home after my parents are gone and I am to pack up their things in boxes, I will not cry. Maybe I will feel scraped clean and open, but not today.

WHY I NEVER MOVED TO NEW YORK CITY

Time is coming for your little town, and it's not going to make it. Its pale scenery will erode, not unlike tombstones slouching helpless towards the earth. The Bi-Lo will become the K-Mart, the furniture outlet, the mattress store, the doggy daycare. I was told the whole strip used to be the family farm of some local author I had never heard of, that his house had been right where the Waffle House now sits. I was told the Walmart used to be ceremonial Cherokee land, constructed despite some tepid protests. When I was a kid, I remember birds flying around the metal beams of the ceiling while we shopped, permanent interlopers from the garden center that I'm sure were shitting on everything. There was a McDonald's in the back, across from the dairy section, complete with a bench where you could snuggle up to a glossy statue of Ronald McDonald. The birds were boldest there, swooping down onto greasy formica tables to capture discarded fries, everyone talking a little louder over the alien din of their chattering. My daughter's Walmart doesn't have birds, or a welcoming plastic clown with his arm outstretched and waiting, and no one ever says that they miss them.

Your town is something you draw with your finger in the patch of dirt during recess while the other kids race and sweat like dogs. The bell rings and you dust your hands off, leaving behind the little mounds of dirt, the intimate etchings determined by the size and shape of you. There is a chance you will return tomorrow and find it untouched, that when you do you will obliterate it with your clean, pink palm, that you will stomp it under the heel of your new sneaker, that you will sail past it, a stranger, on your way to the swings. I was driving through the indistinguishable stretch between south Georgia and north Florida where you must presume that every puddle hides an alligator and that every stop is a sundown town. I passed a little main street that had a VHS rental store, and to my knowledge Blockbuster had been bankrupt for two years. What time does not take it renders indecipherable and sun-bleached, the ghostly blues and greens of the plastic VHS covers crowding the window.

You will be indigestible to your town, no matter how many times it may try to consume you. You will hope to be its hacking cough, its red and feverish splinter, the very bite it chokes on. When I had finally compiled every piece of the outfit I needed to dress like Judd Nelson from *The Breakfast Club*, it was July. The missing article had been the perfect gray overcoat, which I found that day at the thrift store and convinced my mother to buy. She pointed out that it neither fit me, the coat being a man's medium and myself being a scrawny eleven years, and that it was summer. As my mother did her shopping, I sat on the patio furniture displayed at the front of the K-Mart, donned in my new coat, sweating, and silently spewing flames. I could feel myself growing more powerful with each questioning look, each snicker, each person who flowed past. You will want to set the whole place on fire, but it's all green wood and wet leaves and smoke.

You are the only real person in your town. There is no culture here and the only place to drink is Applebee's. Every parking lot has a car with a hood you can smoke on. The whole town is one big parking lot, and you are the night and the full moon above it, forever. Before I graduated high school, my friends all started talking about where they would go to college, the general consensus being anywhere but the south. My voice was the trance like honestly of a hypnosis patient when I told them I was never going to leave. They cried: Bible belt, red state, bad politics, worse people! But the town's obligatory prayer times have taught me to keep my eyes open, tilt my head back, and study the water stains on the ceiling. To catch the gaze of the others with their eyes wide open. Here I can be Charon, delivering whoever needs it past the blithe violence of the political roadside signs. Here I am the director of an oblivious and unwilling play. Here I can find the clarity of thought you meet on the walk home, in the brief darkness between two streetlights.

You cannot escape time, she will find you. But she does prefer to overnight in towns where the motels still have smoking rooms and the only people walking are the people with nowhere to go. I wait for her here. When she comes to me, we sit across from each other in a booth, in the back of the bar. The wood paneling is fake and the candle on the wall is an LED and there is a freckle on her left ear lobe and I want to bite it. We are playing footsie, five finger flay, we are screaming at each other, we are kissing softly, we are staring blank faced at the baseball game on the big screen. I light her cigarette and she regards me as though from a great distance, Cassiopeia to termite.

"It's nothing personal," she says, "when I tell you it's over."

And I never wanted to be here, anyways, but her smile is the hot adrenaline of a childhood dare. I could stay, if it would prove her wrong. I smile back and pay her tab. I step outside and into the warm bath of night. There is the sound of cicadas competing with the buzz of a neon sign, there is a flyer on the ground advertising discount tires, there is the smell of rain. I stand on the curb and I wait ten minutes, and I wait ten minutes, and I wait.

ANDREW HAHN
I AM THE GOD

ANDREW HAHN WRITES AT THE CROSSROADS OF DESIRE, FAITH, AND SURVIVAL. HIS CHAPBOOK *GOD'S BOY* **(SIBLING RIVALRY PRESS) QUEERS THE CHRISTIAN MASCULINE WITH A FIERCE AND UNAPOLOGETIC EYE, TURNING WORSHIP AND ABSENCE INTO WILD, INTIMATE SONG. HE RECEIVED HIS MFA AT VERMONT COLLEGE OF FINE ARTS AND SERVED AS THE WRITER-IN-RESIDENCE AT RANDOLPH COLLEGE IN LYNCHBURG, VIRGINIA. HIS WORK HAS APPEARED IN** *HOBART PULP*, *BARREN MAGAZINE*, *THE FLORIDA REVIEW*, *CRAB CREEK REVIEW*, **AND OTHER SPACES. HIS POEMS LEAN TOWARD THE ECSTATIC AND THE DANGEROUS, REMINDING US THAT THE BODY IS SCRIPTURE, LUST IS PRAYER, AND SURVIVAL ITSELF IS ART. HE NOW LIVES IN RICHMOND, VIRGINIA. READ HIS WORK AT ANDREWHAHN.ME**

GOD'S BOYS' BILL OF RIGHTS

1. Every boy must serve God and God alone, and if a boy discontinues service, he may be subject to eternal torment.

2. Every boy will be cared for by God and disciplined appropriately as defined by the Bible.

3. Every boy will be surveilled at all times for God is all-seeing and all-knowing.

4. Every boy must submit to God's will, with the understanding that painful or unpleasant experience is in accordance with God's sovereignty and in the boy's best interest.

5. No boy shall lust after a man other than God, for God is all-knowing, and if a boy lusts, he may be disciplined appropriately as defined by the Bible.

6. No boy shall have the final word, but may pray wholeheartedly for God to consider whatever the request shall be.

7. Every boy shall expect God to push him in faith and obedience, to force him to create new limits and boundaries in subservience to God's will.

8. Every boy that experiences pleasure at the hand of God shall refer to it as God's love, and every boy that experiences pain or discomfort at the hand of God shall refer to it as their sinful nature.

9. Every boy will experience pleasure at the hand of God.

10. Every boy will believe they have experienced true and unconditional love.

GOD'S BOY LEAVES HEAVEN

heaven is a long way to fall
for those who were chosen
& he chose me   I served
my God day & night   behind
the temple veil where his way was my way
my Yahweh   the only way
his portion   my prize
tied to a bed like hanging from a cross

men hate it when your desires become your own

heaven is so small when viewed from earth
the ego of a man who thinks the world wants him   who
every day   as I walk the blue ridge trails   sends
signals   & messengers   & demons   to turn me toward
righteous paths   he's so obsessed w me

men hate it when they can't have what they want

I could never fully walk away from God   for once
godliness met my tongue
I understood what it felt like to be worshiped   to be a man
to hold the creator of the universe in the palm of my hand

IMAGE: WORSHIPPER

I try to remember the days without worship
but I can't   some men are cursed
to toil in the fields   others are born
to fill the ego & find comfort in the rod
& staff

I left God   yet I still worship
a peach ripens & rots on a countertop
a dog harvests food
I am what I have always been whether I was born
or bred

if man is made in the image of God should I
not also give them what is theirs   dominion
over the earth

but I too am made in the image   the boy to stroke
God's ego   what is it that God wants from me

I left God   yet He still calls
Yet His nights are lonelier still   I've been told
God does not need us   what a gift to be alive
but God gets lonely too
if He didn't   why are we here
why the promise of heaven
why the yearning calls of a man   a God   so great

WHERE IS GOD IN THIS

the poetry of human
sickness, the stained eyes of men
searching for softness

SERMON FOR THE LOWLY

1 Truly I tell you, if a man seeks or
uses another to fill his own spirit,
then he has given himself away.
2 Likewise, if the vessel understands
the exchange, he is under no obligation
to return, for what has been given to him
was given for selfish gain.
3 In this way, the giver
becomes subservient to the receiver
and the receiver may no longer kiss
the feet of his superior,
4 and if he does, he must not tell
the giver of the power he holds because
it no longer belongs to him,
5 and the receiver may use it as he sees
fit without consequences, because of
the spirit in which it was given.

IMAGE: SINNER

I am made in the image of God
I am made in the image of God
I am made in the image of God
I am sucking off a father in his car
I am biting an apple off his family tree
I am raising his son as my own
I am swallowing the sons he'll never have
I am God the son
I am God the son
I am God the son
I am praying worse things happen to you
I am the demon in the dark corner of your conscience
I am inching us toward oblivion
I am praying for violence against myself
I am praying for a more interesting life
I am praying for my brain chemistry to decide who I am
who I am
who am I
I am the great I Am
I am the great I am
I am the self-existent God, the God who's always been there
I am the God who has been sent to you
I am the God who empowers the bitter alpha
I am the God you sacrifice your life to fuck
I am the God who created you in my image
& I am the God who despises you for it

loving you is like the first bite of summer peach
the sticky sweet of summer maple in the corner of lips
the revenge of being alive   of sucking your tongue as
bass destroys my heart   of your hand in my back pocket
walking down cary street

the satisfaction of surviving long enough

to know this is exactly

what God intended

GOD'S CURSE

I can now enjoy the beauty of creation   free
from expectations of servitude   the blackwater
creek trail & waterfall at hollins mill
the fruits and vegetables grown from a man's love
a stray kitten's glowing eyes in the sewer grate

if this is God's curse   so be it

was this world more beautiful in God's arms   I can't
remember from so high up   I can't remember
for God so loved the world He kept his secrets
                                                                        like me
in the absence of His light

when He cursed the earth He couldn't have known
a God who never suffers is not a God who understands beauty
every time I am moved by creation   I think not of heaven
& its riches, not of my duties & pleasures in the Lord   I think

how beautiful to be where God is not
how beautiful to be here on this earth

FINAL PRAYER

Dear God   I can't do this anymore
I don't understand that what I've known my whole life
can be so contrary to who You are

I'm sorry

sometimes a boy finds himself sewn
among rocky soil   & his roots gets choked
I know this wasn't Your plan
it wasn't mine either

you see God   I have found
unconditional love in a man who won't live forever
& it makes love more precious
for You   boys live & die
& come back as choked seedlings
who cannot provide breath for another living thing
like we did for You

I'm sorry

You showed me wonders   I saw Your face
& survived   I saw Your face when I believed You
loved me   I believed
every word You sang with the voice of a choir
I soared on the wings of Your tongue
but vanished in the darkness of Your throat

I have seen the wonders of the earth
& gazed upon the face of the waters
& the backs of mountains   the resilience
of humankind   my kind   & where
were You   were You
in the man's touch   in the air
we shared   in the life he planned
on the good soil

You were nowhere

You see God   I have to go
for I am just a boy to You
but You   once   were everything to me

BARUCH PORRAS HERNANDEZ

BE FAT! DO CRIMES!

BARUCH PORRAS HERNANDEZ IS THE AUTHOR OF THE SMALL POETRY COLLECTIONS *I MISS YOU, DELICATE* **AND** *LOVERS OF THE DEEP FRIED CIRCLE* **FROM SIBLING RIVALRY PRESS, AND HAS BEEN PUBLISHED IN ENTANGLEMENTS LIKE** *SLUTS, SPLIT THIS ROCK, THE RACKET, FOGLIFTER, ASSARACUS, THE TUSK, BOLD ITALIC, WRITE BLOODY*, **AND MANY MORE! HIS SOLO SHOW** *LOVE IN THE TIME OF PIÑATAS* **WON "BEST SOLO COMEDY" AT THE NEW YORK CITY FRINGE FESTIVAL IN 2025. HE HAS RECEIVED FELLOWSHIPS AND TAKEN PART IN RESIDENCIES FROM BANFF CENTER FOR THE ARTS, BERKELEY REP, CAROLYNE MOORE WRITERS HOUSE, AND THE LAMBDA LITERARY FOUNDATION. HE'S PERFORMED HIS WORK ALL OVER NORTH AMERICA INCLUDING SHOWS WITH** *THE RUMPUS, BUSBOYS AND POETS, SF SKETCHFEST, RADAR PRODUCTIONS, WRITERS WITH DRINKS*, **AND** *LITQUAKE* **AND IS A TWO-TIME WINNER OF** *LITERARY DEATH MATCH*. **HE HAS PROBABLY MADE OUT WITH YOUR DAD, AND LIVES IN SAN FRANCISCO WHERE HE IS A REGULAR HOST OF LITERARY SHOWS FOR KQED.**

THE BOTTOM AVATAR STATE

Did you gays know,
that getting wildly fucked
can give you
an astronomically great hair day?!

The other day this top fucked me
so good, and for so long, that at
one point I started crying *I'd leave my husband*
for you! I'd leave my husband for you!
You have a husband? he asked,
NO! But If I did, I would LEAVE him
for YOU! When I left this man's house
I felt like I had just walked out a goddamn salon!
I was a fucking Vidal Sassoon commercial!
My eyes, sparkling! My skin, glowing!
Time stopped enough for me to take 127 selfies
AND THEY ALL LOOKED GOOD!

At one point, when the top was hitting me
with multiple orgasms my eyes started
glowing
suddenly I became
connected
to every bottom in the universe.
I saw

everything.

Felt the orgasm of every bottom
getting fucked around the world
at the same time.
Became one
with the Bottom Spermcelium network,
the Ass Astral plane, if you will.
I had entered the Bottom Avatar State
—my soul   pure peace—
I saw
the beginning of time   the first cave bottom
getting his caveback blown out

fucked like a naughty, naughty cave whore.
I saw
the future   when the bottoms of the
Last LazyBear on Mars 3069
all have space orgasms at the same time
during the last orgy of humanity
before the gargantuan Cosmic Space Octopus
size of a galaxy
swallows our solar system
ending all human life in our world!
                                But then I also saw
the Cosmic Space Octopus now full of
oh so much! — future gay space jizz, it
DEEvelops a thirst for DICK
so it finds a bigger
Dom Top Daddy Space Octopus
that gives it a wild interdimensional fucking
beyond human comprehension for 3000 years.
When they both cum at the same time,
the explosion is so massive it restarts the universe
letting life begin anew.

When I am asked while on a panel for artists
what advice I would give to young queer men?
My advice is always
Bottom Sooner.
My advice to any straight man
at any time is always
Bottom sooner. Evolution, or your god
put a magic button in your manpussy that can
connect you to the universe.
You want to see God?
Slide a cock up your butt.

As a bottom I have learned;

Gay jizz
          we have been
Gay jizz
          we are
Gay jizz
          we will be.

SONG TO THE MOON OR DATING WHILE GAY AND LONELY

Plenty of fish in the sea, plenty of fish, the sea
is big, don't give up on love, my friends say, no,
don't give up,
        there are plenty of Men in the sea, my friend
said, PLENTY of men in the sea!, which made me
automatically picture

        hundreds of men, up to their necks in the darkest
of waters, deep empty night, barely hanging on for dear life,
exhausted from treading water in the middle of the ocean,
I'm the only one on a small boat, sitting on a throne
of donuts and burritos, the men beg, they plead, weep
for me to help them, and I,

I just let them all drown....

then sing a song to the biggest mother fucking full moon
you have ever seen
in your mother fucking gay life.

OUT! DAMN SPOT! OUT, I SAY!

Freshmen year of high school this girl
came to school with a toothpaste stain
on her jean jacket,
everyone thought it was cum
so everyone called her Cumstain
    for an entire semester.

We learned a lesson that year,
that the littlest thing can change your whole life,
but only if you let it.
Anyone can endure a semester of ridicule
to come out stronger at the end of that tunnel

and that you really should be careful
when rubbing one out cause
that poor girl,
was me...

and yes it was cum.

BE FAT, DO CRIMES

Whenever I break a chair
just by sitting on it,
I think to myself, wow
MY BODY IS POWERFUL.

I bend gravity as I walk! Feel the earth
groan a little when I plant my feet on it.

I crack mirrors when I look at them
because they are not enough
to hold my beauty!

Calling all mountaineers! Time to climb me
like the sex mountain I am! Get on fellas!
Big Foot is real, you found me! Gargantuan!
The beast of your dreams! Planetary!
Enough to feed a village! A couch you can fuck!
A bed that will massage your back
as you melt on top of me, a donut
between both our mouths!

I know skinny jerks hate it when I say this:
My sex life got better after I got fat.
I'll say it again, for the back of the room:
My Sex Life Got Better AFTER I GOT FAT!

One lover says I make him feel like a real person,
one lover says no one can make him cum as hard as I can,
one lover keeps coming back, says I devour him
like a meal, and I do, from his ear lobes to his delicious toes.

Here comes the behemoth, get the fuck out my way!
Oh no, you bought an airplane seat next to me? Get ready to cuddle, bitch!
My legs, my skin, my softness abounding
astronomical, my ass astounding.
I have swallowed Jonah. He was delicious!
I have swallowed the wooden marionette
and his little old man too!

When I have troubles   I eat a donut,
fuck a beautiful man,
and forget.

Be Fat!   Do Crimes!
Commit the crime of walking
down the street while being fat
with a smile on your face, I promise you
it will just ruin the fuck out
of skinny people's days.

All the men on the sex apps in San Francisco,
a choir of headless bodies screaming:
"I am Into: Jocks! Muscle! Daddies! Twinks!
College! Nerd! Trans! Otters! Fit! Any Race!
Guys Next Door! Older! Younger! Kink! Poz! PnP!
Discreet! Monogamous! Polyamorous! Pissplay! Footplay!
PUPPYPLAY! Sir-Boy! Father-Son! Uncle-Nephew!
Bisexual! Bukkake! Lampshades! Cars! Couches!
Corn on the Cob! Towels! Curtains! Elbows! Trees! Carrots!
Desks! Sculptures Made of Thumbtacks! Anything,
Anything, WILL FUCK ANYTHING but please
for the love of god, don't BE FAT!
No offense, it's just a preference,
if I take care of my body, so should you."

But I don't care. All I have to do
lift my arms at a Bear event
and all the men start salivating
when my shirt raises over my gut.

At a sex club I run through the twinks like a
lion runs through tall grass and reeds.
They climb on top of me like Totoro as I
fly through the gay air. At the sex party seven men
get on their knees to form an ass buffet.
My tongue, mightier than the sword!
Where is the beef? Here I am!
To Me, My X-Tra Large Men!

Sometimes I have sex just because I know

somewhere some hateful twink is furious
that a fat person is loving their life. I know
my orgasms are so great somewhere
a skinny bitch feels the cosmic energy of my release
and screams in jealous agony
  and to that I say
"Oh honey,
    go have a snack."

after the shooting, he asks, what would you do
if you had to face these people that want us queers dead, that want
drag queens, and trans people dead?
that night, I didn't know what to say,

GO AHEAD

Kill me, and thousands of boys will wake up singing,
yearning to kiss another boy, kill me, and ten thousand more
will fall in love, kill me, and more men all around the world
will become brave enough to make love to another man,
many more will hold hands in the daylight,
become drunk with lust and love. Kill me,
and queer elders will hold their lifelong partners
even closer to their chests as they fall asleep.

Kill me, and the earth will bloom,
covered with young men kissing,
smiling as it turns bursting with love.

Queer love is the spark other planets can see
from earth in the dark.

Queer love never dies,
kill us, and 100s of years in the future, queer hands
will still sway in the air dancing, triumphant, joyful,
spinning long after no one remembers
who the fuck you are!

CHEEK TO CHEEK

Have you ever been,
face deep in a man's ass
and suddenly gotten very depressed?

I have.

You know something is wrong when
you get hit with a wave of uncontrollable sadness
right in the middle of doing something you love.

One minute you're tongue deep in his butthole
the next minute you're thinking—what,
is the meaning of it all?
Why, am I working so hard? I live in San Francisco, I'm
never going to own property!

No matter how hard I tried to concentrate on
his delicious butthole, the thoughts just kept coming
the earth is dying,
a racist orange bag of puke was able to become president
twice!
have any of the men in my life actually loved me?
did I love them, or were we going through the motions?
I'm never ever going to be able to do a cartwheel!
no matter how hard I try!

Not to get too personal, but
just between us gurls
while face deep in this guy's butt,
I started crying.
I've never wanted to use a man's buttcheeks
to wipe away my tears,
but I'm glad they were there.
The guy noticed something was up,
turned slightly and asked,
Is everything okay? 'cause gay men are polite.
I said *everything is fine.* Talk about masking your feelings!
Look, I'm an immigrant, we work hard, and I had a job to do
so like a gay little fish from a Pixar movie, I sang to myself

Just keep rimming, just keep rimming,
    just keep rimming rimming rimming!

and got back to work! Fucking him with my tongue,
spanking his butt hard and jerking him off from behind.
I got so into it, I accidentally gave him, according to him,
one of the best orgasms of his life, hands free
his joy sprayed all over my sheets,

and you know what...
I felt SO MUCH BETTER!

GHOSTS OR MEN

I do not believe in ghosts.

My mother's house is haunted.

Knives fly off my mother's counter
after she's gone to sleep. I google
the scientific explanation for objects
that move by themselves at night.
I hear footsteps in her hallway, knocking
from inside closets that are empty once
I thrust the doors open. Cupboards open
by themselves slowly. I hear walking on
her roof,
It's the neighbor's cat! my mother says,
You need more sleep.
Your house is haunted, mother!
Oh well, she says, *Drive me to Target!*

In her living room, while we watch tv,
we both are startled when my phone flies
off her coffee table and clunks on the floor
by itself.
How did you do that? my mother asks.
I didn't do that! I scream
There are ghosts in your house, mother,
aren't you concerned!?

My mother says,
I'm not worried about ghosts.
I'm alive,
they're dead.
I win.
Besides, ghosts don't scare me at all.
At least
they're not
men.

LA PEQUEÑA MUERTE

If you've never held
your best friend's hand
while both on your knees
as you each go down
on a fatass D,
are you even friends?

The answer is NO!

My therapist once said
I thiiiiink
you're addicted to self-sabotage.
I said *I thiiiink you're right*
we should definitely have sex!

During the pandemic I went to the dentist.
It was nice to have someone put
their fingers in my mouth again. At one point
my dentist pulled a hair out of my mouth
that she said had been wedged
in my gums for who knows how long.
The dental assistant tried to make me feel better.
She said *oh don't feel bad, my husband has a beard*
and he gets hair stuck between his teeth all the time,
then my dentist said, *Yes, but this hair is red,*
it doesn't look like it belongs to you.

I once had an orgasm that opened up
a door to other dimensions,
I knew my weak meaty boney body
could not pass through the portal,
but it was nice to be able
to catch a glimpse of the other realms.
I once orgasmed so hard
I swear I felt my queer ancestors
spirit high fiving me from the dead worlds.
I once made my first boyfriend
cum so hard the old ladies next door called
the police and told them that

a woman with a high-pitched voice
was getting murdered and calling for her father.
I once had an orgasm so intense
that I flew out of my body, up into the air,
saw the sky, saw the city, the roof of the sex club
I was in. I floated down and saw my body shaking
with my eyes closed and my hands gripping
the bottom's hips for dear life,
I slowly got back into my body and started to breathe.
I don't know if it was a very good orgasm
or I had a very small heart attack
and almost died. Either way
I had an out of body experience.
I did start going to the gym after that.

I hope my great grandkids don't want
to be at my death bed when I go, 'cause
if I make it that far, and can still jerk it,
I'm going to want to orgasm as I leave this earth.
That seems like the best way to go.

LAYING DOWN WITH MEN

My 72-year-old Mexican father talking to the server
during brunch with my brother and me,

Yes, these are my two sons,
one is gay, one is straight, but he does Jiu Jitsu,
which means both of my sons love to rub themselves
up against sweaty men.

My brother says *Yeah, but Dad, I actually win gold medals for it.*

To that I say, *Sure, but Dad I actually make the men have orgasms,*
and then they buy me dinner, what does my brother give them?
Ring worm?
No thank you!

The server, *I'll bring you guys the check!*

SUNDAY AT THE EAGLE WITH 69 MEN NAMED GEORGE

A hot little 25-year-old otter with the mandatory mustache
and the septum piercing walks up to me
on a hot day at the Eagle
Baruch! I'm so glad I ran into you! You are like my slut hero!
I look up to you! I wanted to let you know,
I just had a 13-man gang bang! Aren't you impressed?
I said *Of course I am! I am so proud of you!*

... I didn't have the heart to tell him
I was less impressed that he was able to be
a cum dump for 13 different tops
but more impressed that he was able to get
13 different gay men to agree on a time and place to meet,
to have all those men actually show up, and not flake.
Now THAT is IMPRESSIVE!

I can't get three gay friends to agree on a brunch date
and not cancel.
So yeah, *Mama! Kudos for saying that. For spilling!*
And for getting all that D,
next time go for 23!

Then I hugged him, told him how proud I was of him,
we smoked pot, and danced with 69 shirtless men
under the gay San Francisco sun. We each kissed
every single one.

AMIR RABIYAH
STRENGTH IN REDEFINITION

AMIR RABIYAH IS A POET, WRITER, AND LIBRARIAN CURRENTLY RESIDING IN PENNSYLVANIA. THEIR WORK HAS BEEN PUBLISHED IN NUMEROUS JOURNALS AND ANTHOLOGIES. THEY ARE THE AUTHOR OF *PRAYERS FOR MY 17TH CHROMOSOME*. **THIS DEBUT COLLECTION WAS A FINALIST FOR THE PUBLISHING TRIANGLE AWARD AND AN ALA OVER THE RAINBOW PICK. THEY WERE ALSO THE CO-EDITOR OF** *WRITING THE WALLS DOWN: A CONVERGENCE OF LGBTQ VOICES*.

CARTOGRAPHERS

I.
We were born, that is the first miracle. Then we were taught to dream of futures,
until those futures did not contain us or reflect us. Until we found ourselves alone, without a map.
We became inventors, then slowly ripened into cartographers. We crafted our own maps.

We created courses as we took to the skies. Etched the lines with our tongues. Shaped worlds inside of worlds. Made fluid borders. Became fluid borders. So gaze. Fix upon the miracle of us.

II.
What is tomorrow, when you are told you cannot exist?
It isn't easy is an understatement. Take your hands. Your tongue. Shut your eyes. Take a breath. Let it go. A kite. Watch it dance in the air. Unseen forces are lifting its tail.

Gusts.

That is us. Tracing our own contours of belonging. Making estuaries our tears, embedding them back into our maps. So gaze. Fix upon the miracle of us.

III.
Full circle. Mourn. Moon. Light. Our future is not only in the stars, but also in our electric fingertips. We wave our hands and light new countries—we thunder our new names, and huddle in the darkening expanse. We laugh with our chosen families, and tectonic plates shift.

IV.
We've gotta become lightning now. When we're gone, someone without a map will fix upon a flashing sky and believe they are loved. They will recognize a chorus of us singing their praises inside of thunder. They will fix on their own hands and know, too, they are cartographers.

WHEN THE DUST SETTLES

You opened your arms for the forgotten ones,
the discarded & misunderstood.
You showed them a mother's love,
enveloped them in a delicate
and powerful embrace.

Beautiful star,
when the dust settles, we'll always remember
how you showed us how to fight
even while the jagged blade of sorrow
pressed on us, to fight ceaselessly.

You said, when the dust settles
I hope my girls will be okay.
You cried out from the cells of Attica
and outside Stonewall's battered streets.
Do you hear me? Are you listening?

How many more of us have to die?
Your heart bigger than any cage.
Even in the midst of so much loss,
you remind us to dream,
to hold tomorrow between our lips.

You remind us, we deserve to kiss without fear.
We deserve to grow old,
to sway our hips if we choose to,
to wear what we wish.

We deserve slow mornings with our lovers,
to relish in the pleasure of our bodies.
Mother Major, we thank you.
How you fed us, when we hungered for visibility
the seeds you planted continue to grow
into a blooming song.

Mother Major, we honor you.
When the dust settles, we will raise our voices,
just as you have always done, in glorious proclamation
and we will let everyone know—
We are still here!
We are still here!

COMING

Two lovers, splayed across the grass
light-streaked rivers
or bones of boats caressing the water
moaning towards the shore
conjugating kisses
mouths blessing one another's necks
into wet vowels, pressing
their hands into folds of the giving earth

Two lovers, their bodies' edges blurred by sweat
& a quickening desire—lose time and let go
and the trees, the trees,
shake the last of the frost
before the coming of Spring

RELEASE

Blundering through adolescence
antsy to escape locker room brawls
Sometimes the halls of school swallow you
and spitball you against the wall
You learn how to make a fist
before you learn to sift through emotions
The translation of boy or man—*fixed*
cumbersome, leaden, difficult to shift
Are you tired yet?
There comes a time, in the quiet,
where waves of sorrow meet
the shore of possibility
Take off that weighted jacket
& wade into the sea, float on your back
& gaze at the expanse of sky,
cry—let salt commingle with salt
Release Release Release
There is a refuge in vulnerability
Strength in redefinition

VERUM CORPUS

When we first met. We used no words.
Only the language of eyes.
How did you know me so quickly?
I thought you too beautiful for me,
but you cooed I see you, I want, I need
you are my world and that was everything…
you caressed the scars on my chest, the ones my father left.
Soon, I told you: how he raised his sword and plunged it into me,
how he screamed "You're no son of mine,"

Hail, true body
Whose pierced side
Flowed with water and blood

I became a swan and flew into the heavens.
Dropped down and found you.
May it be for us a taste of things to come

Once I was yours, I became what you willed.
You wanted a horse. I became your steed.
I shrank. I thanked. I'd plead. And thanked.

Who knew the toll this war would take?
The violence began again. An eruption. Broken plates. Bruises.

In the trial of death, you left me.

Strangers coming home found me.
Strangers sang my spirit back to me—they fed my light.

Hail true body, which having truly suffered

Hail the body which returns to its truest state.
In dying, I returned. In dying, I created myself whole.

UP/RISING INTO

Oh child,
not everyone will understand
the grief of losing
all you hold, dear
friends, schools, homes, some connections disappear

You tire of swimming upstream
outside, the sidewalks teem with upcoming elections
officials debate your right to exhale
ban books
& the poetry of your becoming

Though you may wish to let go, know

You are beloved!
You are beloved!
You are beloved!

Another season will arrive
& welcome you
so, go on now
open your hands
let jasmine fall from your palms
follow the trail of petals
leading you towards a precious life

Let the wind whisk you
take flight
up/rising into gender euphoria

Your joy self-made
a present
a future
transcendent

DINNER WITH BUZZ ALDRIN

When I met him, he was a rehearsal of a man—all jawbone, crushing handshake & toothpaste smile. It had been two days since the accident & the pain tore through my atmosphere. Father insisted I go out & put on my pretty white dress. I tried not to fidget through the throbbing, while they laughed, smoked, gawked at women & talked about the elections. I tried to sit still, but I had so many questions.

Mr. Aldrin, what's it like up in space, to see us as a sphere, just a ball of magic spinning?

What's it like to gaze at us outside of us? Mr. Aldrin?

What does it feel like to be weightless? Mr Aldrin?

I waited for his answer like I waited for God's voice in church. *I want to give you something*, he said. He scribbled his autograph & handed me a photograph of himself.

I rubbed my fingers over the gloss.

—so you can show your friends... isn't this super?

When I got home, the remains of my science project were still strewn on the patio, and my blood had dried. My wind tunnel, still only half constructed & the wings I started to carve when the knife slipped, grounded, flightless. I unwrapped the soaked bandage. The inner workings of my hand exposed themselves. The monacled moon cast light through our stratosphere. My body was ablaze with injury.

That night, I discovered a whole other world under the surface of my skin.

/TRACTIVE

Have you ever seen the moon's reflection from underneath the surface of the water? Have you ever seen the colors come to life? What once looked translucent green becomes a dark blue, black, or purple, or nameless. Your eyes bewilder you, as light streams in lines, trickles, bursts, and glows. Beams shards of dusty krill, & scales, & bubbles.

Have you ever swum in the ocean at night? Stripped off your clothes & run in shouting? We have heard you do this. We have listened to you laughing. We swam towards you to listen to your joy—your pores dilate, to hear the water glide over your skin. For a moment, you forgot you didn't have gills; you understood the mathematics of Oneness as being part of a chain of interconnected sparks of life.

Do you know what the moon says to the sea at night? The moon– she pulls & tugs at the sea. She says, *"We are two pieces of a puzzle that must join."*

The sea says: *"Draw me closer to your dry mouth, let me wet you with mine."*

Did you know the moon is in love with the sea? This has been the case since the beginning. They cannot bear to be apart, so they dance together at night, with stars as witnesses, a passion incomparable. They dance during the daytime with the sun watching over them, warming the sea. The earth cannot contain the sea, nor prevent the moon & the sea from being together.

Love has its highs & lows, so the tide heaves and hoes.

As We travel We sing to the moon, knowing the sea is the womb of the earth. We have seen all the ways the moon appears from underneath. We know the moon's caress. We remember what We sing to one another. If you, too, ever come to know this, remember Us, Our bodies consumed by light as We emerge.

THE PLANET

As for the heart, it changes, the heart
knows how to protect us into a hardened state,
a frozen lake we traverse, expect cracking
& then iced dunk chatter teeth, temperature

drop into sleep, to…
next station final stop, please disembark. Or
that planetary mass, can whirl us closer to surrender, to…
the scroll of a beloved's hair, the ink of a beloved's hair

when ink meets the oxygen of color's night.
My little planet fantasizes palpitation. Vessels swim
in the salt of my blood. Some days, they only travel
towards the shores of a kiss.

Take my planet out from my ocean, and it becomes
a thing of horror, magic without gills, a fish away
from its origin, flailing in protest, before being placed
in an ice chest, or held up by hands in victory.

But for now, I am grateful for my little planet. No person
has successfully stuck their flag in its dust, nor claimed
it as their possession. Each day, I say thank you, axis.
My little planet captains me towards a vast

language away   from the safety of the lighthouse.

AMIR'S NOTES ON THESE POEMS

Many of the pieces I have included were explicitly written to be set to music. One of my close friends, Mari Valverde, is a trans Latina composer. She reached out to me many years ago to put my poem, "Our Dangerous Sweetness," to music. Since then, she has reached out to me numerous times to write a poem on a specific theme or subject, and she then wrote the music and vocal arrangements. She subsequently introduced me to Saunder Choi, another composer, who has also requested that I write original poetry to be set to music.

When the Dust Settles was an original poem I composed for Mari Valverde to set to music. It was commissioned by the Peninsula Women's Chorus and premiered in 2020. I had the honor of speaking with Miss Major and conducting an interview with her. Some phrases, such as "When the dust settles," and "we are still here," are direct quotes, while others are paraphrased. Additionally, Miss Major said she loved the theme song from the 1980 film *Somewhere in Time*. I listened to this song on a loop while writing this poem.

Coming: I was commissioned to write this erotic poem around the theme of "Spring" by Cantus Vocal Ensemble in 2022. Mari Valverde composed the piece, titled "Before Spring."

Release was a poem commissioned by the California All-State Tenor Bass Choir and was composed by Saunder Choi. Saunder reached out to me and asked me to write a piece exploring gender. The piece was specifically written with cis-teenage boys in mind, since those were the members of the choir. The piece was selected for the Arkansas All-State Choir auditions, but when one Arkansas legislator found out I, the author of this poem, was transgender, he had it removed. The *Arkansas Times* wrote an about it; you can find on their website. [Editor's note: As a lifelong resident of Arkansas, it was very important for me to include this particular piece in *Assaracus*. This act of censorship and erasure was directly responsible for my decision to bring *Assaracus* back into print. - Bryan]

Verum Corpus: The Windy City Performing Arts commissioned "Verum Corpus" in celebration of their 40th year. It was composed by Saunder Choi. The text is inspired by the story of Caeneus, a mythological hero from Ovid's *Metamorphosis*. I wanted this piece to discuss abuse within the queer community, isolation from biological family, and finding healing within chosen family.

Dinner with Buzz Aldrin is based on a true story. Ask me about it sometime.

Up/Rising Into was commissioned by Seattle Pro-Musica in 2024 and premiered in Seattle in 2025. I wrote this poem as a love poem for transgender youth because of the current climate we are living in, and the hundreds of anti-trans bills that are being proposed, many of which are being successfully passed across the United States.

The Planet was inspired by the poetry collection *Behind My Eyes* by Li-Young Lee.

MEGAN VOLPERT

BRUNCH BRACKET 12: THE JOANS

MEGAN VOLPERT'S PURPOSE IS TO GIVE GOOD GUIDANCE. SHE CREATES SACRED SPACES WHERE CHARISMA, UNIQUENESS, NERVE, AND TALENT CAN THRIVE. SHE IS AUTHOR OR EDITOR OF OVER A DOZEN BOOKS ON POPULAR CULTURE, INCLUDING TWO LAMBDA LITERARY AWARD FINALISTS AND AN AMERICAN LIBRARY ASSOCIATION HONOREE. HER NEWEST WORK IS *WHY ALANIS MORISSETTE MATTERS* **(UNIVERSITY OF TEXAS PRESS, 2025) AND SHE WON GEORGIA AUTHOR OF THE YEAR FOR** *BOSS BROAD* **(SIBLING RIVALRY PRESS, 2019). IN ADDITION TO HER INTEGRATIVE MEDICINE PRACTICE, VOLPERT'S OTHER GIGS INCLUDE TEACHING AT REINHARDT AND KENNESAW STATE UNIVERSITIES, BEING A FELLOW AT THE AMERICAN INSTITUTE FOR PHILOSOPHICAL AND CULTURAL THOUGHT, AND WRITING FOR** *POPMATTERS* **AND** *SALON***.**

OBVIOUSLY, THESE BRUNCHES NEVER HAPPENED. ANY RESEMBLANCE TO PERSONS LIVING OR DEAD IS A PURELY SPECULATIVE RESULT OF MY IMAGINATION. - MV

1. JOAN JETT

She swags in carrying a tea tray of room temperature Pop-Tarts, some frosted and some not. Joan has commandeered a conference room and arranged a half dozen chairs in a row like a sofa. Her fuck you often reads a lot like fuck me, but I can't be tempted when she tells me she read that thing I wrote about her and it wasn't bad. We talk about some rock documentaries, and she agrees when I say the s'mores Pop-Tarts are my favorite and chuckles when I tell her about how my college roomie always used to have them waiting for me when I got home from class after dark. Joan didn't get the s'mores ones because they didn't seem brunch appropriate and her sentence trails off in an indication that our meeting like this may not be an isolated incident. We smoke and she offers up some pool time. At first I think she means we're going swimming on the roof, but then it turns out she means billiards and then it turns out she means a video game. She whoops my ass but doesn't talk any shit about it. I try to make clear I didn't lose on purpose and we are wonderfully suspicious of each other. There are other people milling around—lugging equipment, arranging coffee cups, shuffling papers—but we have each other's attention. The sun is beginning to set when I leave. Joan side-hugs me before I stand up and someone in her entourage lets out a tiny gasp.

2. JOAN BAEZ

As we're walking in the door, I ask my wife how long she thinks the conversation can go before anyone mentions Bob Dylan. We set the over-under at fifteen minutes. Joan is on the phone when we sit down. It sounds like the person on the other end is crying and they are talking about a terminally ill feline. She motions to us to enjoy the entertainment, which is a little old lady in a *sí se puede* apron making fresh guacamole tableside. Minus the time on the phone, it takes twenty-five minutes before somebody says the name. Her pivot from ancient to modern politics is so fast and smooth we almost didn't notice she'd moved on to the new Gaza issues, which are the same as twenty years ago. She does most of the talking and plates keep arriving even though nobody actually placed an order. A three-piece mariachi band inches its way toward our table and when they're right behind her she finally turns around and asks if they know some song I've never heard of. Their leader nods enthusiastically and Joan gets up to sing with them for a minute, until it's clear the violin is winging it and the tune kind of collapses in on itself at the bridge when Joan sits back down. The margaritas are top notch and as we're leaving, she is asking us to sign up for an environmental thing she's doing with Bonnie Raitt, which we probably will because it's hard to say no to such a pushy auntie.

3. JONI MITCHELL

It's a jungle in Laurel Canyon. Everyone is talking to the people they already know and the main gossip relates to the Iowa Writers' Workshop, how it's either a scam or a shame. These are music people whispering about a mid-career author who finally worked up courage to do a book on Joni only to put so much of his own neuroses on display that the result fell flat. These musicians blame Iowa; nobody asks Joni what she thinks because it's understood that such matters don't interest her. A few people huddle around her, she in the big chair and them at her knees, on ottomans and overstuffed floor pillows. I make a plate and settle on a tufted stool shaped like a turtle. Joni is quiet, occasionally tapping her cane on the hardwood. Each time she strikes the floor it runs right through the turtle and up my spine, this Morse code her way of connecting with me as I contentedly pick at my snacks and listen. After a half hour or so, her head swivels almost imperceptibly in my direction and she mutters, "like your gator. Hospitable." She crooks one finger toward the brass alligator topping my cane. I nod in thanks and say "ditto" to the silver bear atop hers. She later looks at me across the room at the door and thumps twice against the floor with enough fervor to turn the attention of the prattlers. The alligator hammers my reply.

4. JOAN ARMATRADING

The dogs weave around our ankles as we go from room to room and it slowly dawns on me, they're named for heavy metal icons—Halford, Hetfield, Ozzy, and Lou—but I don't comment on it. Joan, Commander of the British Empire, might know as much about murder mystery novels as she knows about playing a twelve-string and we talk about who done it for over an hour. She has never seen *Ten Things I Hate About You* but has amusing thoughts on *The Tempest*. Mindy and Maggie are meanwhile in the garden picking herbs for omelets, also producing out of season plantains from nowhere. While we were all in the kitchen, there was a fair amount of singing—Cyndi Lauper giving way to Van Morrison and the original London cast recording for the musical *Hair*, where the fun temporarily died down as we all realized how much the 1979 movie soundtrack deviates from the 1968 album. I also confessed, only because she asked, that "Drop the Pilot" is my favorite among her singles. She nods and shrugs that that's what most Americans will say, and I can feel her disappointment, not in me but in the ongoing obscurity of her B-sides even among those of us who care. I think because I did not ask for a tour of Bumpkin Studio or the room with most of the guitars, Joan taught me her secret recipe for the world's fluffiest blueberry scones, and I'll take it to my grave.

5. LADY GAGA

I don't often go to the Upper West Side, but Stephanie Joanne Angelina Germanotta is insisting we meet at Joanne Trattoria. All this hinges on a technicality and when I sit down, Gaga acknowledges the same. Your list was on my list, she winks. This is one more way she can stay in tune with her dearly departed namesake aunt, just like the album, tour, tattoo, this restaurant. We're doing eggs benny with Canadian bacon and brioche French toast with fruit, two coffees apiece and we trade plates halfway through. We talk briefly about Rilke and her admiration is greater than mine, then at more length about Sedgwick where my admiration is greater than hers, which highlights our five-year age gap. I learn everything she knows about Joanne's poetry and painting. I learn Gaga dismisses reviews of her work but devours academic treatments of it. When I try to clarify this will be poetry, not theory, she clucks she knows my other projects and thus doesn't believe me. I'm flattered beyond repair. This leads to a Sicilian Margherita pizza and tiramisu, and we vacate with leftovers in hand just as the drag queens are setting up their 6:30 show. She offers me a car, but I walk four blocks along the park back to the 72nd Street station because I want time to process, and after saying yes to everything about this event I just felt like lobbing one good no at the end of it.

6. JOAN CRAWFORD

We arrived early to ensure everything was exactly as Joan's team requested. Two floral arrangements that were off got whisked away into the kitchen and the rest was correct. Every visible member of the waitstaff tensed as the clock struck. We sat up straight and tried to breathe. Ten minutes rolled into fifteen. Eyes across the dining room began searching each other for signs. It did not take so long to come thirty-seven stories down the elevator from the top floor suite of the Fontainebleau. We dared not order anything, but at half past, someone silently placed a basket of bread. When the clock struck again, all sunk instantly into a lukewarm disappointment-relief. Joan did not appear to be coming, though no one from her team had yet said so. They did end up calling the kitchen, and then some darling young lady came out to break it to us with the dressed oyster course already in hand—pink pineapple, jalapeño and Baïka caviar. It hardly went with our coffee, but Joan had set the menu and everyone was determined to make the most of their overtime. So it was a parade: the cold bar tower they reserved for her just in case, the Caesar salad, a New York strip and porcini risotto, sides of mashed potatoes and asparagus béarnaise, a gigantic baked Alaska and of course a wine pairing for each of these plates that we took single sips from out of politeness. Joan paid.

7. JOAN CUSACK

She brings out the Chicago in me. We're dropping f-bombs all over the lakefront as we bicycle to our destination, and in the crush of mid-morning bike lane traffic we miss the breakfast menu by fifteen minutes. Joan says it's never too early for a hot dog, so we pedal to the nearest Skip's. She's got eighteen years on me but is less winded than I am when we arrive. It's also not too early for chocolate shakes and we settle into a hard booth by the window. We bond over neither of us liking sport peppers and both of us having degrees in English from midwestern schools. She tells me that she bikes this path pretty frequently and confesses, with apologies for slightly alluding to job stuff, that her bicycle playlist starts with Carly Simon's "Let the River Run." Even though *Working Girl* is set in Manhattan, the song is pure Chi-town to Joan. We're both hopped up on shake sugar and humming the opening bars, and by the second mention of New Jerusalem, she's got it playing from her phone and we are singing it at the top of our lungs. There are no other customers and the two guys in the kitchen come out to see the ruckus. They realize it's Joan and start snapping photos. She stands up on the booth seat, dancing and waving. It's all over four minutes later. Everyone is ecstatic and the kitchen sends us out a free order of pizza puffs.

8. JOAN FONTAINE

A letter from an unknown woman left me with suspicion. A million to one this Rebecca was a damsel in distress. But since you can't beat love and you gotta stay happy, the sky giant said I'll be seeing you. Our Le Cordon Bleu hostess made her signature chicken Fontaine, pan-fried with lemon juice and zest, capers and a dash of sherry. She made me want to call it a day. No bed of roses, no more ladies, the users, the women, the witches offering a serenade that promised a voyage to the bottom of the sea, some music for madame, the emperor waltz. They wanted something to live for from this day forward until they sail to an island in the sun. When Jane Eyre called for our September affair, ready to showcase her famous curried tomatoes, beyond a reasonable doubt I stood in for her man of conquest as the man who found himself. The constant nymph had a certain smile, like the lion in winter. She claimed she simply needed tea and sympathy, but this above all, she begged, kiss the blood off my hands. Perhaps she was not born to be bad after all, and tender is the night where poison ivy grows. Yet in the light that failed, in the dark mansions into which she led me full of private lives and radio voices that sparkled forty carats, I was nothing more than a severed head, one more bone thrown by Olivia.

9. JOAN RIVERS

The invite said if we hate the place there's a good deli around the block we can go to afterward. Everything came on slate plates, and Joan kept exclaiming how gorgeous they were until I feared she might stuff one in her giant handbag. The side of veggies was yellow and orange, and she preferred it to the kale because what even is kale and green wouldn't look as nice against the slate and she was dead sure the carrots would be cut like flowers. She'll eat anything in the shape of a flower but cut off your lesbian jokes at the knees. A man can order a few different plates, no questions asked, but if a woman orders nineteen or twenty things, she's a glutton. Joan lives on Cool Whip. Really it was all I could do to keep her from going dessert first. It was a pie shaped to give an illusion of Beef Wellington and Joan got another one to take home, so she has at least one thing in common with Elizabeth Taylor, which is that their favorite food is seconds. All the guests were liberals but she weaseled one surprise fascist in there to make it a better party. Although Joan famously cannot cook, let it never be said that she can't dish. We all mourn in our own way and I mourned the end of this brunch by having a great steak for dinner on the slate she slipped into my handbag.

10. JOAN OF ARC

Joan ordered the second largest charcuterie board on the menu and asked for wheat bread instead of multigrain crackers. I'm averse to cheese that isn't melted, so I noshed on two of the meats a bit and left the rest to her. She ate almost nothing, just picking at the edges of the board, but she downed two sweet teas in a half hour. In short, she ate like a nineteen-year-old. Most of the meal was packed up and given out to a few homeless folks we met outside in the alley behind the restaurant. There was another girl about her age, a server having a smoke break next to the dumpster. The girl complimented her pants and Joan went right up and talked to her for fully fifteen minutes about the joy of pants. They really were gorgeous though, a rough, red-dyed linen that was heavy enough to drape well but still be breezy, and well-tailored for her scrawny shape. Just three brunettes gabbing about fashion until Joan lifted up her shirt to show the girl that they were embroidered with mustard fleurs-de-lis on the two butt pockets, and we both winced at the thick scars across her lower back. I bummed a cigarette in silent commiseration. The server then showed off her own stainless steel two-finger ring that had little spikes poking up at the knuckles. Joan thought it was genius and asked to try it on. The girl told her to keep it.

11. JOAN HOLLOWAY

These tend to run more like business meetings that happen to have good breakfast spreads. A pack of cigarettes keeps us on pace and the meeting is over when the pack is empty, usually two and a half hours. Each of us takes notes by hand in a notebook that fits in a pocket. We smoke between little dishes of berries and baskets of biscuits. Our coffee is half half-and-half, no sugar. One of us is always cold and the other is always sweaty, so we dress in layers. Joan goes for reds and greens for obvious reasons, while I go for a mix of shades of black that keeps neighboring eyes from lingering on our table too long. At this table, everyone gets what they need, which is time to kvetch about having to follow idiotic orders from inferior men who have failed upward and to give each other wise counsel concerning our next batch of entrepreneurial schemes. Neither of us ever brings up the baby or romance. This is a commiseration that otherwise knows no bounds and we get deep into the momentum of it in a way that alerts any server that ours is not a table for small talk. Spare us your weather. We are talking about money, roads, futures, prospects for leverage and the decay of time. We are actioning like men and proud but cautious about the fact that this horrifies them. Joan and I are not fantasizing; we are world-building.

12. JOAN DIDION

My anger only comes now when I summon it, no pop-ins. Most of it has been converted into grief, which springs up suddenly and overstays inconveniently. When I sit down, I ask Joan if she can help move the grief, tell me secrets to digesting it. She makes a low bark like laughing and dashes my hope of easement. Further, she taps and scratches her pointer finger on the live wood table edge, pinning down an irony: she was likewise hoping I could tell her how to convert anxiety into something useful and now she worries I can't help with her worrying. But I believe I can and outline some healing practices. She sends back her eggs because she deems them undercooked and then tells me I'd fit right in on the woo woo west coast, which I find insulting—the west coast part. This reminds me to ask if she's heard Diane Keaton's now out of circulation narration of *Slouching Towards Bethlehem*. Joan hides a knowing smile behind a demure sip from her teacup, nodding and waiting for me to say the thing. The thing is Keaton's very annoying way of pronouncing "San Bernardino" with such a hard R. She does it maybe a hundred times. Nobody says it like that, and it is not charming. Joan shrugs in noncommittal agreement, speculates whether this is the key to Keaton's entire oeuvre. Neither of us knows the relation between this frustration, grief and anxiety. We keep our sunglasses on.

IAN YOUNG
SOME YELLOW LEAVES: POEMS OLD & NEW

IAN YOUNG WAS BORN IN LONDON IN 1945. HIS FIRST "PROFESSIONAL" PUBLICATION WAS IN THE HOMOPHILE MAGAZINE *ONE* **IN 1967. SINCE THEN HE HAS PUBLISHED POETRY, BIBLIOGRAPHY, FICTION, LITERARY JOURNALISM, AND A PSYCHOHISTORICAL STUDY OF GAY MEN,** *THE STONEWALL EXPERIMENT* **(CASSELL). ALONG THE WAY HE HAS BEEN A PUBLISHER, A BOOKSELLER, AND A DISTRIBUTION SUPERVISOR FOR A DAILY NEWSPAPER. HIS MOST RECENT BOOKS ARE** *LONDON SKIN & BONES: THE FINSBURY PARK STORIES* **(SQUARES & REBELS) AND AN EDITION OF OSWELL BLAKESTON'S** *THE COBRA KING* **(WRY PRESS). HE LIVES IN TORONTO WITH HIS PARTNER WULF HIGGINS, A THEATRICAL PROPS MAKER.**

CHILD OF THE SEA: A REVERY

for Ken Yukich

Sea island sun in the silver wind,
sun island sea at day,
sailor are you a man or a child
when you drown in the deep bay?
Landlord of the Sea,
today I read your words
from Coral Island,
dropped from the white gull's
yellow beak
to my right hand.
And I could read,
stretched here upon the sand
your scroll of seaweed
from sea-claimed land.
By wet rocks
over bone-white sailors'
sunken bones,
my mind is cold.
Caresses of the waves
wash my mind. My body
in the caves
is wet and tastes
of salt
and sailors' graves.
"Send boats for me.
I sign this Landlord of the Sea."

I know the sea has no lord
nor are the waves
ruled from any island.
Only a boy or a sailor once thought so.
Only a boy and a sailor think it so.
No sun in the sea at the ocean's heart,
No sun at the cold sea floor.
I would send boats
but I have no boats
to carry you to the shore.

JUST BEFORE DAWN

for Tony Wilson

There are some friendships
speech will not allow, that live
in gesture and silent beauty—
or fall apart.

I came across you weeping
in the darkness. No words
could fathom
what chill being entered you then,
whispering from your warm mouth
into my puzzled kiss
with the sound the wind makes
in cold grass.

You faced me, silent
as a crypt, devoid of questions,
cupping a stranger with my name
in your pale hands.

Now in the stillness
between lightning and thunder
your shaking spirit
hovers,
the moment before dawn.
The torrent of your long hair
drenches the hills.

THE SECRETS OF THE GARDEN LOVE THE DARK

Were I the black moth
that flies by night,
that glimmers in the moonlight
and is gone,
I'd light upon your shrine
and rest awhile,
that potent perfume
dusting my wings.

TWO CATS AND A GHOST

for Kirby Congdon and Ralph Simmons

I am the one-eyed talking cat
that sits on the Hiereus throne
and waits for temple business
to begin,
who crouches
as the figures move about
and only when they stop
comes out.

And I am the fire-eyed stalking cat
who sits
on the garden wall
and pounces
on a moth
and chews its wings
and is not heard
beyond the temple door.

Our mother's bones
rest in the tulip bed
by the garden door.

Our mother's ghost
circles the circling feet
on the temple floor.

DREAMING OF JOE

You were in my dream again last night, Joe,
happy and beautiful
as in the old days.
We met on one of those crooked streets
we used to find.
You were carrying groceries and
wearing my shirt again.

How many years has it been
since you turned away hurrying
to your blind date with Death?
He stood you up I hope. Or did he claim you,
leaving only your happy ghost,
handsome as ever
in my dreaming bed?

AUTUMN WOODS AFTER BOOKHUNTING

for Yuri Cowan

It's a good day for me
when I find a gift to send you—
the right book, found in a trance,
as though the Guide
got through just a little better than usual
for a few moments.

Do you know
those old poems, I wonder—
by Tu Fu, Wang Wei and the rest?
The poet sits outside his mountain home
among the fir trees,
writing a poem
with a delicate brush—
a poem about how he misses his friend
who has gone to a faraway place.
The poet,
no longer young, imagines
he and his friend will be reunited
when they have grown old
and have long grey beards.

Treading through these woods
I feel the air's chill now.
The days are growing shorter.
Kneeling to run my hands
through fallen leaves,
the memory of your hair
at my fingertips,
your kiss
light as a moth
on my crooked lips.

ON THE DEATH OF MARY OLIVER (1935 – 2019)

Always a deep thought
when a great poet dies.
We carry on regardless.
We won't have that companion,
that voice,
with us on the path any more.
Only those words,
those lines in a book,
in the pocket,
acting as guide.

SPIRIT HOUSES

for Bryan Borland

Our spirit house is grey with weathering,
small but imposing
among the trees
at the head of the path.
I suppose they turn out those spirit houses
by the hundreds
in the no-longer mysterious East.
Though I've never seen another one
in operation, as it were,
as far as I can remember.
Passing spirits, they say,
employ these houses,
though what they employ them for
remains something of a mystery.
Rest stops? Surely not.
But these things are beyond me.
Always were.
May your spirit house
remind you of good fortune
and the odd ways of certain passing specters.
You may feel the urge
to provide it with a few wildflowers
now and then.

DEATH OF THE BATHROOM SPIDER

Bathrooms, it seems,
can be hospitable to spiders.
Being spider-friendly,
I don't mind.
Now and then,
I would catch a glimpse
of our own bathroom spider,
spidering about,
black and bristling,
the size of a fingernail—
a frequent visitor.

Every so often,
at intervals of about three weeks,
there would be the bathroom spider,
wandering around
at the bottom of the bath,
apparently stranded.
On these occasions,
she (let's assume she was a she)
had to be rescued
with a napkin
or a sheet of computer paper.

And then, early one morning,
there she was,
not in the bath alas,
but floating on her back in the toilet,
quite dead,
all eight limbs folded and
curled on her sooty thorax,
immaculate,
like a prayer.

I would miss this tiny familiar.
But death by water, it seemed,
was unavoidable.

Days later,
pausing for groceries on a country drive,
I ducked behind the frozen food store
to have a discreet piss.
As I stood in the grassy corner,
I noticed a back bucket
half full of water from the drain pipe.
A large beetle
was struggling to avoid drowning,
all six legs thrashing helplessly.
I cupped a handful of water
with the creature in it,
and placed him (was he a he?) on the ground.
He calmed, and rested a few seconds,
before scuttling away
into the grass.

A fortuitous rescue, as it happened,
lessening, just a bit,
my tiny grief
at the death of the bathroom spider.
After that, the rest of the day went well.

WALKING THE HIGH LINE WITH YOU

Of all New York's pleasures that I recall,
the one I remember best of all
is walking the High Line from end to end
with an old love, or a new friend.

BOYS INSIDE OUT

Inside every bad boy
there's a good boy
trying to get out.

Inside every good boy
there's a bad boy
trying to get out.

Let them out!

**WE FUCK. WE WRITE.
WE MAKE SPACE.
WE LOVE. THIS
IS OUR MAGIC.
THIS IS OUR
THUNDER.**

**THIS POETRY IS FOR
THE ELDERS, THE
FAGS, THE QUEER
KIDS, THE QUIET
ONES, THE QUEENS,
THE DYKES, THE
DOLLS, THE GOOD
TROUBLEMAKERS, &
THE AFTERPARTY.**

BRYAN'S POEM

MY BROTHER'S ASSHOLE

The frame: the shower door slid open.
The view: I have to be four.
Four-year-old bright eyes
outward, from an angle sitting in the tub, just enough
water to cover my legs, the co-conspiracy of brothers,
mine old enough to be left alone with me,
young enough to smile after standing up from
the toilet, bending over, turning his face back to me,
spreading his cheeks and his asshole,
the first asshole I see,
the first asshole of many,
my brother's pink asshole, my brother's secret
doorway to his laughter.

Did anyone else ever see him this way?
The way a little brother
saw his big brother then,
bare butt, dark cave, doorway as open
as the most intimate secret, as adventure,
as dirty and clean
as his humanness, as his boyhood.

Brothers being brothers being brothers,
being art and humor,
and years later lust, but right then love,
and so I chase art and humor and lust and love.

Oh brother, what did you do
but show yourself to me,
but give me something
to remember you by?

www.ingramcontent.com/pod-product-compliance
Lightning Source LLC
LaVergne TN
LVHW052341100826
845147LV00021B/1148

* 9 7 8 1 9 4 3 9 7 7 8 7 1 *